M000158265

THE BRIDGES OF GOD

A Study in the Strategy of Missions

THE BRIDGES OF GOD

A Study in the Strategy of Missions

BY
DONALD ANDERSON McGAVRAN

Wipf & Stock
PUBLISHERS
Eugene, Oregon

Wipf and Stock Publishers
199 W 8th Ave, Suite 3
Eugene, OR 97401

Bridges of God
A Study in the Strategy of Missions
By McGavran, Donald Anderson
ISBN: 1-59752-250-3
Publication date 7/12/2005
Previously published by World Dominion Press, 1955

FOREWORD

The main thesis of this book will not be new to those who have followed the work of the World Dominion Press, particularly in the books published over the names of the Rev. Roland Allen, the Rev. Alexander McLeish and others, in many pamphlets, and in articles in the review *World Dominion*. It has been the task of the Survey Application Trust (World Dominion Press) to devote its attention to working out the meaning of the witness and life of the indigenous Churches throughout the world, and this task it has faithfully pursued for many years. Much of this writing has, it must be confessed, fallen upon deaf ears. Perhaps this is partly due to the fact that the very organization of missions, with their multitude of activities, educational, medical, and social, the "hum of mighty workings", has fascinated us, as the flame fascinates the moth. Perhaps in part it is due to the fact that much current thinking presupposes that the work of evangelization can start again, so to speak, from scratch, whereas the truth is that all engaged in the mission enterprise live in the midst of a situation created partly by themselves, but mostly by the devoted efforts of their predecessors.

In other words, to build on the plain is easier than to build in the city where the ugly erections of former days must be destroyed before something more appropriate can be raised.

It is one merit of Dr McGavran's book, that it does

not ignore this. It deals with the given tasks and with
the state of the Church in the countries which he himself best knows. Facing the scene as it is, he is severe in
his criticism and enthusiastic in his commendations;
these are not faults, but rather advantages. A policy for
missions which has to move for ever in the greys and in
the twilights, in which the great issues do not stand out
in contrast, is no policy at all, but a compromise im-
perilled by all the risks of inaction in a day when
multitudes are in the valley of decision.

Briefly, Dr. McGavran's thesis can be put in one
sentence: it is a contrast between the "People Movement"—to use his own term—and the "Mission Station
Approach". The Mission Station Approach, classic as
has been its place, is essentially a static conception, as
the words themselves witness. Dr McGavran himself
has been a station missionary for a generation. It should
not be inferred that the great work of missionary boards
and societies of the last 150 years, based in the main on
the Mission Station Approach, has not been successful,
or that through this approach great movements of
peoples to Christ have not been initiated. But as the
Church itself has grown, the inadequacy of the static
approach has become evident, so that with every year
the need to clarify our thinking on the meaning of the
indigenous Church becomes more urgent. The conception of the "People Movement" is different. Evangelism is no longer mission-centric but church-centric. It
is not only a conception, which has the sanction of
apostolic example, but it is more fully in accord with
the spirit of the age. It is people that matter, it is movements of people that are significant for the future and,
not least, for the growth of the Church throughout the
world.

Thus, Dr McGavran's book is a tract for the times.
The whole question of the means by which the Church

must expand has become a new and a burning one. The Churches in the East are no longer content to depend on the Churches of the West, nor should they be. At the same time, the countries of Asia are growing rapidly in population; they resent anything they consider to be of foreign origin in the world of ideas and religion; and they dislike, in particular, preaching for conversion to Christ. If the expansion of Christianity in these countries depends on its being a model from the West, then the cause of the Gospel in the world may be given up as lost. But this is not the dilemma the Churches and their missions are required to face. At least, Dr McGavran has given himself the task of showing that, if it is, the fault lies with them.

KENNETH G. GRUBB

November 1954

CONTENTS

ix

CONTENTS

INTRODUCTION

Here is a book which deserves a careful reading by all who are concerned for the world mission of the Church. It is clear that we are entering a new stage in that mission. That stage demands a careful re-study of our message and our methods.

Thus far in the present century we have been following in the main the methods developed in the nineteenth century. That was a day when Western peoples were bringing the rest of the world under their dominion. Their dominion might be political, but increasingly it was also economic and cultural. In vast areas the political rule of Western Europeans has either passed, or is passing, and resentment is vocal against their economic control. Yet with political independence has gone the adoption of much of Western civilization. The day is rapidly passing when, as in the nineteenth century, the missionary can come as a representative of the conquering Occident and when he can be a pioneer in introducing useful elements of Western civilization, such as schools and medicine. Nor can he rule the younger churches as he once did almost of necessity. More and more the younger churches are producing their own leaders. Increasingly the primary assignment of missions is evangelism: the proclamation of the Good News and assisting in the emergence of churches which, rooted in the soil and with their own leaders, will be witnesses to the Good News. All this is now commonplace in missionary circles. Yet we have not faced its full implications in methods. Here is a book which boldly sets forth the issue and makes positive and sweeping proposals for a change in the policies and programme of missions.

The author is no armchair strategist. The son of missionaries to India, he himself has served in that country for nearly a third of a century. He has read widely in the history of missions.

Not all will agree with the diagnosis, the interpretations of history, and the proposals for action which the author puts forward. Were mission boards, missionaries and younger churches to assent to them and to make them a basis for their policies in the years ahead, radical changes would follow. The author frankly recognizes this fact and the objections which he well knows will be raised. He is aware that the changes which he advocates will not come quickly. Inertia, caution and vested interests will serve as a sufficient brake. Moreover, he formulates important questions which he cannot answer and where, as he rightly says, much more research and experimentation are called for.

Yet the procedure set forth is not to be dismissed lightly. It deserves careful study by missionaries, mission boards and younger churches. If we are to meet the challenge of this new day we must be eager to have our minds break open in new ways, to abandon or reduce drastically our accepted methods, and we must resolutely devise and apply new ones. To the thoughtful reader this book will come like a breath of fresh air, stimulating him to challenge inherited programmes and to venture forth courageously on untried paths.

It is one of the most important books on missionary methods that has appeared in many years.

KENNETH SCOTT LATOURETTE,
Professor Emeritus in Yale University

In this book, the following usage has been generally, but by no means exclusively, followed:

Church	The Church throughout the world.
church	A particular denomination.
church	The local church.

The author employs various terms in a special or technical sense which is explained in the text. Capitals have been preserved for the following:

People Movements
Mission Station Approach

To that great host of comrades
whose teaching, preaching and healing
has been blessed by God
to the establishment of the Church
in all the world
this book is affectionately dedicated

THE BRIDGES OF GOD

I

THE CRUCIAL QUESTION IN CHRISTIAN MISSIONS

How do Peoples become Christian?

A great deal of study has been devoted to Christian missions. We have come to know the answers to many questions about mission work. But what is perhaps the most important question of all still awaits an answer. That question is: *How do Peoples become Christian?*

This book asks how clans, tribes, castes, in short how *Peoples* become Christian. Every nation is made up of various layers or strata of society. In many nations each stratum is clearly separated from every other. The individuals in each stratum intermarry chiefly, if not solely, with each other. Their intimate life is therefore limited to their own society, that is, to their own people. They may work with others, they may buy from and sell to the individuals of other societies, but their intimate life is wrapped up with the individuals of their own people. Individuals of one stratum, possibly close neighbours, may become Christians or Communists without that stratum being much concerned. But when individuals of their own kind start becoming Christians, that touches their very lives. How do chain reactions in these strata of society begin? *How do Peoples become Christian?* This is an enquiry which is of enormous concern to both the younger and older churches as they carry out the Great Commission.

This is so partly because of the size of the missionary movement, and must be seen in its full range. A Directory of Churches and Missions in any large non-Christian land shows the names of missionaries on page after page, along with hundreds of pages of names of occupied towns and villages. The missionary enterprise is indeed a vast one. Millions of money for Christian missions enter Asia, Africa or South America each year. These millions have been coming for many years and it may be will come for many more. It is a labour of heroic proportions. Those carrying it on bear a heavy responsibility to the donors to see that it is carried on effectively. For the most part the donors' deepest desire is that as many people as possible become Christian. To see this accomplished, those directing the enterprise need to know how *Peoples* are Christianized. Furthermore, and of supreme importance, is the fact that missionary leaders are servants of Him Who died on the cross that "all nations" might be saved, that the world should come to know of the power of the resurrection. Hence, if they would be honest stewards, if they would carry out the Great Commission, they should not merely "carry on mission work", but should become experts in how both individuals and peoples come to embrace the Christian faith.

It is an inescapable fact to-day that if the world is to be unified it will be so on one of two bases—universal materialism or the Christian faith. There is no other religion or philosophy which by its extension could possibly unify the world. Since we Christians cannot look forward with equanimity to a secular world, we must believe that the basic religious unification of the countries of the world, with all that is implied for their peace and harmony, depends on a further extension and deepening of the Christian fellowship. We believe then that the unification of the countries of the world and the future hope of peace depend greatly on our understanding of the sociological and religious processes by which peoples become Christian, and our acting accordingly.

The world is in a period of cataclysmic change. During this period the shape of things to come is being steadily determined through the interplay of colossal forces. Old civilizations are being revolutionized and society is malleable to an extent not known for centuries. The sense of need is clamant and peoples are looking for a saviour. At such a time as this the Christian Church finds itself firmly planted in practically every country of the world, with church buildings scattered up and down the land in hundreds of thousands of strategic centres, with numerous Christian schools, colleges and hospitals, with a great corps of dedicated missionaries and in most lands a numerous company of national fellow workers. It is difficult to imagine a more strategic disposition of resources. Despite this favourable set-up, however, the Christianization of peoples is not proceeding as it should. After a century and a half of modern missions, less than 1 per cent of the Chinese and less than a $\frac{1}{2}$ per cent of the Japanese have espoused the Christian faith. In India the percentage is only two. In the Muslim world far less than one-tenth of 1 per cent have turned to Christ. How peoples become Christian clearly needs a great deal more study. It evidently does not happen merely by energetically and devoutly carrying on "mission work".

Christian missions in the lands of Asia and Africa are coming to the end of an era. The entire conduct of missions must be thoroughly re-examined. In the minds of too many politically dependent peoples, becoming Christian has been associated with denationalization and with a distasteful dependence upon the dominant whites. How peoples accept Christ in independent countries must be most carefully considered if churches and missions are to meet God's call to help build up these nations.

This book is based on the presupposition of partnership between the older and younger churches in carrying out the Great Commission. Its message is not for Westerners alone, but for other nationals also. All concerned with carrying out our Lord's command should know a great deal more about the process by which peoples become Christian. This book is written in the hope that it will shed light on that process and help direct the attention of those who love the Lord to the highways of the Spirit along which His redemptive Church can advance.

Some Answers Prove Erroneous

The fact of the matter is that there are comparatively few who know much about this subject. There is some speculation about it—probably most of it in error. The reasons which cause peoples to espouse Christianity are sometimes described, but the descriptions do not often stand up under scrutiny.

For example, the secret of growth, some say, lies in the Nevius Method, that is, in employing no paid national workers, in teaching converts tithing and in stressing Bible study. Let us see. The Korean peoples are very like the peoples of China and Japan and like them belong in various degrees of devoutness to the Buddhist and Confucianist religions. In Korea by largely following the Nevius Method a Christward trek was established and hundreds of thousands became Christians. Yet, on the one hand, many a mission has stressed tithing and has taught the Bible conscientiously, and still numbers its Christian community only in hundreds. On the other hand, some missions employ paid agents, do relatively little Bible study because of the illiteracy of their numerous converts, achieve an annual giving per person which is less than 1 per cent of income, and yet number their Christians by hundreds of thousands! Evidently the Nevius Method is not the main answer as to how peoples become Christian.

Some say that great growth is to be expected from work among aboriginal tribes. Let us see. In 1845 several missionaries of the Gossner Evangelical Lutheran mission in Germany landed at Calcutta and made their way overland by ox-cart to the hill country of Chhota Nagpur. They worked among the aboriginal Uraons and Mundas. They had a little group of converts within the first five years and thereafter for fifty years a slow but steady growth. Around the turn of the century they had some major ingatherings. In 1914 the church numbered about 80,000 souls. Then during the First World War all the German missionaries were interned or sent back to Germany. Their church in India was left leaderless. Nevertheless by 1936 the Lutherans numbered 136,000. Here work among aborigines resulted in significant growth.

But on the other hand, about 1880, the Church of England, with all its prestige and resources, through its Church Missionary Society, entered the Mandla District of the Central Provinces in India about 200 miles due west of Chhota Nagpur, and, in country very much like it, worked among the aboriginal Gonds. For sixty years it carried on the Gondwana Mission. It had the advantage of the example of the Lutheran Mission to the east. Yet it never succeeded in starting any kind of a Christward movement among the Gonds. After the withdrawal of the English, Bishop Azariah of Dornakal, who had experienced a very successful Christward movement among the peoples of Hyderabad, sent his own Indian missionaries into this aboriginal field. But no Christianization of the Gond people even started. True, a few hundred individuals from various castes during the seventy years have become Christian, but even these either reverted to Hinduism or moved away, till to-day there are *practically no Christians* in the Mandla District. Evidently carrying on mission work among aborigines is not the chief secret of growth.

Some say that any vigorous mission work carried on for many years will result in great growth. Let us see. In China[1] one American denomination has been at work for eighty years. It has had a missionary force at times of over seventy. It has established some strong Christian institutions in China. Its Chinese leaders have played an honourable part in inter-church affairs during the last thirty years. Yet to-day the churches established by that mission are made up of less than two thousand souls—men, women and children. Evidently many years of faithful devoted work is not the determinative factor in growth.

In Africa, Uganda was reached and missionary work begun against a background of the greatest turmoil and opposition about 1890. To reach Uganda, the early missionaries had to cross Kenya. Both countries were under Britain's influence. Yet note the difference in the rate of growth. In the 63-year period, 1890–1953 over half the population of Uganda, but only 15 per cent of the population of Kenya, became Christian. And, during the 33-year period 1920–53 about 45 per cent of the population of Ruanda-Urundi became Christian. Why has the Christianization of the peoples of these countries, all of them at a similar degree of cultural

[1] This book is being written after the Great Tyranny has banned foreign missions from China. But we shall write as if China were still a mission field. We do not believe that the Church is finished in China. The expansion of the Church there has only begun.

development, proceeded at 60 miles an hour in Ruanda, 30 miles an hour in Uganda and 10 miles an hour in Kenya?

The Correct Answer Must be Discovered

How *do* peoples become Christian? Here is a question to which not speculation but knowledge must urgently be applied. The question is how, in a manner true to the Bible, can a Christward movement be established in some caste, tribe or clan which will, over a period of years, so bring groups of its related families to Christian faith that the whole people is Christianized in a few decades? It is of the utmost importance that the Church should understand how peoples, and not merely individuals, become Christian.

II

THE UNFAMILIAR IN PEOPLE
MOVEMENTS

Individualistic Westerners cannot without special effort grasp how peoples become Christian. The missionary movement is largely staffed by persons from the West or by nationals trained in their ideas, and while evangelization has been carried on with correct enough views on how individuals have become Christian, there have been hazy or even erroneous views on how peoples become Christian.

Western Individualism Obscures Group Processes

In the West Christianization was and is an extremely individualistic process. This is due to various causes. For one thing, Western nations are homogeneous and there are few exclusive sub-societies. Then too, because freedom of conscience exists, one member of a family can become Christian and live as a Christian without being ostracized by the rest of the family. Furthermore, Christianity is regarded as true, even by many who do not profess it. It is considered a good thing to join the Church. A person is admired for taking a stand for Christ. There have been no serious rivals to the Church. Thus individuals are able to make decisions as individuals without severing social bonds.

Again, with the disruption of clan and family life following upon the industrial revolution, Westerners became accustomed to do what appealed to them as individuals. As larger family groupings were broken up through migration, the movement of rural folk to the cities, and repeated shifts of homes, people came to act for themselves without consulting their neighbours or families. A habit of independent decision was established. In the Christian churches this habit was further strengthened by the practice of revival meetings appealing for individual decisions to the accompaniment of great emotion. Indeed, the theological presupposition was not merely that salvation depended on an individual act of faith in Christ (which is unquestioned), but also that this act was somehow of a higher order if it were done against family opinion (which is dubious). Separate individual accessions to the Church were held by some to be not only a better, but the only valid, way of becoming a Christian. Had the question arisen as to how peoples became Christian, the answer would have been given that it was by individual after individual becoming soundly converted.

Of the social organism which *is* a people, or of the desirability of preserving the community life, indeed, of enhancing it through the process of conversion, there tended to be little recognition. Peoples were thought of as aggregates of individuals whose conversion was achieved one by one. The social factor in the conversion of peoples passed unnoticed because peoples were not identified as separate entities.

However, a people is not an aggregation of individuals. In a true people intermarriage and the intimate details of social intercourse take place within the society. In a true people individuals are bound together not merely by common social practices and religious beliefs but by common blood. A true people is a social organism which, by virtue of the fact that its members intermarry very largely within its own confines, becomes a separate race in their minds. Since the human family, except in the individualistic West, is largely made up of such castes, clans and peoples, the Christianization of each nation involves the prior Christianization of its various peoples as peoples.

Because of the intense battle against race prejudice, the concept of separate races of men is discredited in many circles. Missionaries often carry this antipathy to race into their work in tribes and castes who believe themselves to be separate races, marry within their people and have an intense racial consciousness. But to ignore the significance of race hinders Christianization. It makes an enemy of race consciousness, instead of an ally. It does no good to say that tribal peoples ought not to have race prejudice. They do have it and are proud of it. It can be understood and should be made an aid to Christianization.

What To Do and What Not To Do

To Christianize a whole people, the first thing *not* to do is to snatch individuals out of it into a different society. Peoples become Christians where a Christward movement occurs *within that society*. Bishop J. W. Pickett, in his important study *Christ's Way to India's Heart*, says:

> The process of extracting individuals from their setting in Hindu or Moslem communities does not build a Church. On the contrary it rouses antagonism against Christianity and builds barriers against the spread of the Gospel. Moreover, that process has produced many unfortunate, and not a few tragic results in the lives of those most deeply concerned. It has deprived the converts of the values represented by their families and friends and made them dependent for social support to the good life and restraint on evil impulses upon men and women, their colleagues in the Christian faith, with whom they have found it difficult to develop fellowship and a complete sense of community. It has sacrificed much of the convert's evangelistic potentialities by separating him

from his People. It has produced anaemic Churches that know no true leadership and are held together chiefly by common dependence on the mission or the missionary.

Equally obviously the Christianization of a people requires reborn men and women. A mere change of name accomplishes nothing. While the new convert must remain within his people, he must also experience the new birth. "If ye then be risen with Christ, set your affection on things above, not on things on the earth." The power of any People Movement to Christ depends in great measure on the number of truly converted persons in it. We wish to make this quite clear. The Christianization of peoples is not assisted by slighting or forgetting real personal conversion. There is no substitute for justification by faith in Jesus Christ or for the gift of the Holy Spirit.

Thus a Christward movement within a people can either be defeated by extracting the new Christians from their society (i.e. by allowing them to be squeezed out by their non-Christian relatives) or by the non-Christians so dominating the Christians that their new life in Christ is not apparent. An incipient Christward movement can be destroyed by either danger.

The Group Mind and Group Decision

To understand the psychology of the innumerable sub-societies which make up the non-Christian nations, it is essential that the leaders of the churches and missions strive to see life from the point of view of a people, to whom individual action is treachery. Among those who think corporately only a rebel would strike out alone, without consultation and without companions. The individual does not think of himself as a self-sufficient unit, but as a part of the group. His business deals, his children's marriages, his personal problems, or the difficulties he has with his wife are properly settled by group thinking. Peoples become Christian as this group-mind is brought into a life-giving relationship to Jesus as Lord.

It is important to note that the group decision is not the sum of separate individual decisions. The leader makes sure that his followers will follow. The followers make sure that they are not ahead of each other. Husbands sound out wives. Sons pledge their fathers. "Will we as a group move if so-and-so does not come?" is a frequent question. As the group considers becoming Christian, tension mounts and excitement rises. Indeed, a prolonged informal vote-taking is under way. A change of religion involves a community change. Only as its members move together, does change become healthy and constructive.

Groups are usually fissured internally. This has a definite bearing on group decision. If in some town or village there are seventy-six families of a given people, they may be split into several sub-groups. Often such divisions are formed by rivalries between prominent men. Often they are geographical: the lower section of the village as against the upper section. Often they are economic: the landed as opposed to the landless. Often they depend on education, marriage relationships, or attitudes toward custom. Group thinking usually occurs at its best within these sub-groups. A sub-group will often come to decision before the whole. Indeed, a sub-group often furnishes enough social life for it to act alone.

Peoples become Christian as a wave of decision for Christ sweeps through the group mind, involving many individual decisions but being far more than merely their sum. This may be called a chain reaction. Each decision sets off others and the sum total powerfully affects every individual. When conditions are right, not merely each sub-group, but the entire group concerned decides together.

Terms Defined

We call this process a "People Movement". "People" is a more universal word than "tribe", "caste" or "clan". It is more exact than "group". It fits everywhere, therefore in this book we shall speak of People Movements to Christ.

We do not use the term "mass movement". This unfortunate term implies unthinking acceptance of Christ by great masses. While it does fairly represent one aspect of a People Movement—that the group usually numbers many persons—it totally obscures the facts (a) that any one group is usually small in numbers, (b) that each member of the group has usually received much instruction in the Christian faith, and (c) that large numbers are achieved only by the conversion of a series of small groups over a period of years. The term "mass movement" should never be used. It obscures and distorts what is really going on.

Stages in Christianization

Two separate stages in the establishment of a Christian civilization must be defined. Although they are closely inter-related it will help to call each stage by a separate name. For our terms we go directly to the Bible, where, in Matthew xxviii 19, 20, we are commanded firstly to "make disciples of all nations", and secondly, to "teach them to observe all things". The Greek word is really "disciple", so throughout this book we shall use the verb "disciple" as a technical term. The Greek word translated "nation" in the English Bible means exactly "people" in the sense in which we are using that term. It does not mean a modern nation like France or China or

Mexico. Thus the Greek means "Disciple the Peoples".

As a first step, then, according to the Great Commission, the peoples are to be discipled. Negatively, a people is discipled when the claim of polytheism, idolatry, fetishism or any other man-made religion on its corporate loyalty is eliminated. Positively, a people is discipled when its individuals feel united around Jesus Christ as Lord and Saviour, believe themselves to be members of His Church, and realize that "our folk are Christians, our book is the Bible, and our house of worship is the church". Such a reorientation of the life of the social organism around the Lord Jesus Christ will be followed by ethical changes. Once Christ is placed at the centre of the life of any community, once He is enthroned in the hearts of the persons who make it up, once the Bible is accepted as the Word of God, ethical and spiritual changes of a high order will inevitably follow. But these changes are not a necessary part of discipling. They are a necessary part of the second step. *The removal of distracting divisive sinful gods and spirits and ideas from the corporate life of the people and putting Christ at the centre on the Throne, this we call discipling.* Discipling is the essential first stage. Much else must, however, follow.

Discipling is definitely helped by the depth of consecration and the completeness of conversion of the individual. The Christian stature of the people cannot rise above that of its individual members. To be sure, Christ will not be fully understood by all the members of the group. The Church was founded by a group of men who for some years after Pentecost made the grievous mistake of thinking that the Lord Jesus was the Saviour of the Jews only. In discipling, the full understanding of Christ is not the all-important factor, which is simply that He be recognized by the community as their sole spiritual Sovereign.

Moreover, the discipling of a people takes place only on new ground. It does not take place in a nominally Christian land. For example, the conversion of ten thousand individuals in an evangelistic campaign in London is not the discipling of a people. The peoples of Britain were discipled centuries ago. The conversion of each new generation is a continuing task of the churches, but it is not the discipling of the British peoples.

The discipling of peoples is often hindered or actually stopped because, in the very first stage, the church leader requires evidence of an ethical change or dedication to Jesus Christ which some Christians in the older churches have not yet achieved. Emphatically both ethical change and dedication will come in due time, provided that the old idols are cast away and the community thinks of the Bible as "our Book", Jesus Christ as "our Lord", receives adequate Biblical instruction, and is led into the habitual worship of God. But such growth is not an essential part of the first stage.

The second stage in the establishment of a Christian civilization is "teaching them all things". For the sake of convenience we shall condense these words into another term and say that the second stage is that of *Perfecting the People*. This is a bringing about of an ethical change in the discipled group, an increasing achievement of a thoroughly Christian way of life for the community as a whole, and the conversion of the individuals making up each generation as they come to the age of decision. All that great effort of the churches in old-established "Christian" civilizations, which deals with holy living and with social, racial and political justice is part of the process of perfecting. So also is all that prayer and labour which is dedicated to bringing millions of individuals, generation after generation, into a vital and personal relationship with Jesus Christ.

As Canon Max Warren points out in his description of revival in Ruanda, "first there was a period when people flooded into the Church for a variety of reasons. . . Then came the stirrings of revival." Had the missionaries refused to let people flood in and be "prosaically prepared" for membership unless they manifested the full joy of revival, the latter revivals of a thousand congregations could not have taken place. Discipling is one thing, perfecting is another.

This point gains importance because many a Christian leader confuses perfecting for discipling. Distinguishing these two stages is essential for those who lead peoples to become Christian. The second stage overlaps the first, but it cannot precede it without destroying it.

We shall occasionally use the word "Christianization" in a popular general sense, to describe the Christian task as it looks to those not holding the People Movement point of view, or alternatively when we mean the whole task of discipling plus perfecting.

For Western individualistic Christian thinkers the new unfamiliar factor in all this lies in the fact that there is a social factor which must be taken into account when peoples are being discipled. In leading peoples to become Christian the Church must aim to win individuals in their corporate life. The steady goal must be the Christianization of *the entire fabric which is the people*, or large enough parts of it that the social life of the individual is not destroyed.

III

PEOPLES AND THE NEW TESTAMENT CHURCH

The New Testament records how large segments of one people, the Jews, became Christian and how from that new Christian society Christward movements in other peoples began. On both counts the story of those first People Movements to Christ is one of absorbing interest to all engaged in Christian missions. That first discipling was certainly a successful one, and can be highly instructive for us because it illustrates aptly what is actually going on in many peoples to-day. Hence it must be studied from this viewpoint. To think of the early churches as People Movement churches will be new to many. But our evidence is that of the New Testament itself.

The Mighty People Movement Within Judaism

At the time of Christ the Jews had a very highly developed people-consciousness. They were full of "race prejudice". They thought of themselves not merely as a people, but as the People of God, the Chosen People. They strictly forbade any intermarriage with Gentiles. They had "no dealings with Samaritans", even though the latter were a kindred people. They were as caste-conscious as are the castes of India to-day. It is essential to realize that, when the Christian Movement started to grow on the day of Pentecost, it was a movement of these people-conscious Jews only. The Lord Jesus

Christ was thought of as a Jewish figure. He had lived as a Jew. The early Church was made up of Jews only. It was a one-people Church for some years. It could have been nothing else.

When the Christian Church started to grow after Pentecost, it is of the highest importance to remember that it was a movement of great numbers. When the Holy Spirit first descended the most remarkable manifestation was that the little Church without hesitation baptized "about three thousand souls" in a single day. This faith and audacity are seldom appreciated. To-day the characteristic answer to groups of a few score seeking baptism is: "Wait and be instructed and tested". But, filled with the Holy Spirit, that first, little, weak Church immediately accepted and baptized *on that day* about *three thousand souls*. There was excellent reason for this guidance of the Holy Spirit. A mighty People Movement had to start with the simultaneous conversion of huge numbers so that each Christian came into the Church with some of his kindred, leaders whom he could follow, families whose opinions he respected, homes where he felt like one of the family, a public opinion which he respected, and a corporate worship which thrilled him. The fact that *a large enough segment of the Jewish people became Christian soon determined the entire course of Christian development.*

The extensive nature of the People Movement to Christ is not often recognized though it is clearly stated in the New Testament. It started with a large group— about a hundred and twenty adults not counting their children and dependents. Pentecost swept in about three thousand more. Within a short time the number of men Christians had risen to five thousand. After that, it is recorded that, "More than ever believers were added to the Lord, *multitudes* of both men and women."[1]

[1] Acts v. 14.

A chapter later we read that "the number of the disciples multiplied greatly in Jerusalem and a great many of the priests (Levites) were obedient to the faith."

In chapter eight "multitudes" in Samaria "gave heed to what was said by Philip" and "were baptized, both men and women". This stress on multitudes and women occurs several times and is important. Families came in, not individual men. That chains of families were converted in Samaria enabled a Christward movement to gain strength in that sub-society of the Hebrews. Probably Samaritans continued for some years to intermarry only with Samaritans, even after they had accepted Jesus as Messiah. At the beginning no Jewish Christian would have thought it proper to give a daughter to the Samaritans, even to such as had become followers of Christ. Had only a few Samaritans come in as individuals they would have had a wretched time amongst the Jewish Christians. But since multitudes of both men and women were baptized there was no social difficulty over marriage.

Among both Samaritan and Jewish Christians not only could marriage arrangements be made and marriages solemnized in accordance with time-honoured precedents, but all the other social necessities could be readily satisfied by those who became Christian. There could be no effective ostracism. This was not because the rulers felt kindly toward the Christians. It was because so many had become Christians that ostracism was impossible. In case of death, there were plenty of Christians to dig the grave and carry out the corpse. In cases of sickness, there were plenty of Christians who had some knowledge of the medicine of that day, and plenty of Christian neighbours who would come in as home folks and help in the nursing. In case of business arrangements the Christian could go to some brother in Christ who would help him. We have only

[solemniz] celebrated

to contrast this situation with that customary in some mission fields, where converted individuals have had to face terrific social boycotts and deprivations, to recognize what an incalculable advantage it was to the early Christian movement that *multitudes early became Christians.*

Peoples protect themselves against infection by a process similar to that which the human body uses. If germs invade the body through a cut or abrasion, the body walls off the infection. A people deals with an invasion of new ideas or practices in just that fashion. It walls off and walls out infected individuals. Ostracism is a people's defence against any new thing felt seriously to endanger the community life. In severe ostracism social intercourse is cut off. No one will give the new convert fire, water or food. If a convert falls ill, his former intimates will have nothing to do with him. He can die for all they care. In fact, they say: "He is dead. He has left us." The most successful answer to ostracism is the conversion of chains of families. The lone convert is particularly susceptible to boycott. But after the first big groups have accepted Christ, ostracism becomes difficult. Christian movements against which ostracism can be used grow slowly if at all. Christian movements against which ostracism cannot be used are able to grow rapidly.

The numbers recorded in the book of Acts were not numbers of unrelated individuals, like those who might be swept into the Church in some great city-wide revival in Toronto or Tokyo. Whole towns and family groups moved into the Christian faith at once. There were some Christian Jews at Lydda. Peter was touring amongst the Christian churches in Judea. He came to Lydda and cured Aeneas. Then "all that dwelt at Lydda and Sharon saw him and turned to the Lord". Two villages were baptized in one day—all their residents became Christians. They preserved their social structure entire. The village elders remained the leaders. Relationships remained undisturbed. There is no record of any social reforms being required or achieved as a part of becoming Christian. In these villages there must have been many who neither understood much of Christ, nor were ready to yield Him sufficient allegiance to go contrary to their groups. Yet they all became Christians. They had been discipled. The centre of their corporate life was now Christ. Perfecting could follow.

This People Movement among the Jews spread rapidly among relatives. It was not confined rigorously to them, as the case of the Ethiopian eunuch and other instances show, but from the day that Andrew found his brother onward, those became Christian who already had family members in the fold. The known relatives of the three thousand of Pentecost must have numbered scores of thousands. The synagogue communities around the Mediterranean were made up of fairly recent *émigrés* who married back into the Palestinian Hebrew community and who had many connections with Jerusalem. It is certain, therefore, that in many a Jewish synagogue all over the Roman Empire there was within two years after Pentecost at least one person who could say: "Yes, I know we Jews are following a new way. My second cousin, my aunt, my wife's uncle are now known as followers of Jesus of Nazareth. They say He rose from the dead and is the expected Messiah." How this enormous number of relatives increased with every group coming into the Christian Church can readily be appreciated.

With every new accession not only did the numbers of persons with one or two Christian relatives increase, but individual Jews began to find that they had large numbers of Christian relatives. A Jew named Joshua might, for example, first hear that his wife's sister's family had become Christian; and then that his own mother's brother's family, including some of Joshua's first cousins, had followed in the Christian way. Then he hears that his own sister and her husband and her husband's parents have accepted Jesus as Messiah. Would not the cumulative effect on Joshua be tremendous? Joshua is typical of the average man in a society where there is a Christward movement afoot. The peoples which make up the nations of Indonesia, China, India, Japan and Africa keep track of relatives very much more carefully than do individualistic Westerners. Relationships are known more accurately and over greater distances. In such societies movements gather enormous power as relative after relative becomes Christian.

Yet becoming a Christian also meant leaving relatives. Every such decision involved separation from those not yet convinced: "A man against his father and a daughter against her mother." What produced this dividing force was not merely individual conviction. It was individual conviction heated hot in a glowing group movement in a human chain reaction. Very few individuals standing alone could renounce father and mother and kinsmen. But reinforced by the burning faith that *our people are following the new way*, such fathers and mothers and kinsmen as refused to follow the Messiah could be renounced. There were heartbreaks and tears, the parting was tremendously difficult, but to men borne forward on the wave of group action it was possible.

The early Church grew *within* Judaism. For at least a decade the Jews who were becoming Christians were not conscious at all of joining a non-Jewish religion. Had they dreamed that this was a possibility many of them would never have become Christians. Even after they were changed by fellowship with the Living Christ, they refused to accept Gentile Christians as full members of the Jewish Christian people! The bearing of this on the growth of People Movements to-day is significant. It shows that peoples become Christian fastest when least change of race or clan is involved. When it is felt that "we are moving with our people and those who have not come now will come later", then the Church grows most vigorously.

The Unplanned Greek Movement at Antioch

The New Testament record is not confined to the growth of a Christward movement in one people. It tells how Christward movements were initiated in other peoples.

The conversion of Cornelius and the Italians with him did not, as far as the record tells, start a People Movement. It was the sort of conversion which could have begun a movement. A large group came in at once. There was no ostracism. The movement could readily proceed among the Italian people since Cornelius and his soldiers and kinsmen and friends were doubtless in effective living contact with their relatives. But a movement does not seem to have originated. The reason may have been that Cornelius was an army man and subject to transfer with his regiment. He was not in close physical contact with his relatives. It would seem that to start a movement the group converted should be in both physical and social contact with its unconverted fellows.

It was at Antioch that the fire first jumped across racial lines causing a Greek movement to arise out of the Jewish People movement. We are not told why a Greek Christian movement started in Antioch. It was not because Paul was there. He was at Tarsus. Possibly there was some Jewish Christian leader at Antioch who had caught a vision of the universality of Christ. More likely, the coming to Christ of the Greeks at Antioch was unplanned and depended on the burning faith of some unknown Christians who were organically linked with both Jews and Greeks, thus forming a bridge between the two peoples. Indeed, this is the hypothesis which is supported by the record in Acts xi.

Because of the persecution which arose over Stephen, the disciples were scattered abroad. Some went to Cyprus and Antioch. As they journeyed they spoke "the word to none but Jews", as was the common custom of Christians at that time. Some of these refugees from Jerusalem were "men of Cyprus and Cyrene". It seems reasonable to assume that, like Nicolaus of Antioch itself (Acts vi, 5), at least some of them were proselytes, i.e. Greeks who had become Jews. They therefore had in Antioch and nearby towns many relatives who were Greeks. Possibly some of these relatives were also converts to Judaism, but most of them must have been uncircumcised Greeks. It was to some of these relatives that the refugees from Jerusalem went, and, departing from the common custom, spoke "proclaiming the Lord Jesus". *This bond of relationship was the bridge over which the faith passed.*

There was a synagogue at Antioch with its quota of Greek proselytes. In view of Nicolaus we may reasonably conjecture that some of these resident Greek Jews had become Christian. These had many Greek relatives of whom by far the largest part must have been uncircumcised Greeks. Thus in Antioch for both the Jerusalem refugees and the resident Christians we have bridges of relationship into the Greek people.

As first one and then another of these socially related Greek groups in Antioch were converted, the conversion of each one making the conversion of the next more likely, there came to be a large community of Greek

Christians there. (Acts xi, 21 and 24.) The Hebrew-Greek Christian church became so big and presented so many problems that Barnabas went up to Tarsus and brought down Saul who was probably known as one who had convictions concerning the conversion of the Gentiles. For a whole year they met with the Greek and Hebrew Christians and taught them. Thus in Antioch also we see the familiar pattern of peoples becoming Christian: the process starts with a considerable number of Greek converts within a comparatively short time.

This first Gentile movement was unplanned, just as People Movements to-day usually are. The leadership in Jerusalem did not intend to convert large numbers of Greeks at Antioch. After the fire was lit, they sent Barnabas there to tend it. This too should be, and usually is, the role played by missions serving People Movements to-day. They follow fires which light "of themselves". Such spontaneous growth is, to be sure, a testimony to the life of the Christian Churches. But in the purpose of God, as the New Testament shows, the further expansion of the Gospel was not to be left to spontaneous unintentional growth. God had a better plan.

Planned Expansion of the Jewish Christian Movement

It was Paul who consciously determined to transform the unplanned outreach to the Gentiles into planned Christian movements among both the Jews and the Greeks. Paul's own thinking must have been greatly influenced by that year with a church of Greeks and Hebrews worshipping together as "Christians". He must have realized that this could be induced in many synagogue communities, and that the true Israel was made up of those who, regardless of racial background, had entered into the new life-giving relationship with

Christ. True, his basic convictions went back to his conversion, at which time he was commissioned "to preach Christ among the Gentiles" (Gal. i. 16; Acts xxvi, 17). Yet there is no record of his converting Gentiles or of forming Gentile Christian churches till after the Antioch experience. Did he try for some years in Arabia to win Gentiles who had no Jewish connections whatever—and fail? Was he trying to win such Gentiles in Tarsus when he was called to Antioch? We do not know. But we do know that immediately after that formative year at Antioch he started winning Gentiles to Christ in large numbers. In that year Paul saw *how* he was going to carry out his commission. He was shown *which* Gentiles the Holy Spirit had prepared for conversion, and how the Jewish Movement to Christ was the bridge across which the Christian Faith could spread to the Greeks. He extended and multiplied these People Movements—both the large Jewish movement, and the very small Greek movement at that time visible chiefly to the eye of faith. We can learn much about how peoples become Christian from this intentional planned campaign of Paul's.

Paul lived for one consuming purpose, that of knowing Jesus Christ and bringing others into the redeemed fellowship. His intellectual achievements and his mystical awareness of God were both tremendous. He wrote with such penetrating light that each succeeding generation has been his debtor. Yet neither his dedication nor his communion with God in Christ was the sole secret of his amazing success. That lay in the combination of his deep understanding of, and fellowship with, the living Christ, with his intuitive and unerring co-operation with God in the extension of these vast stirrings of the peoples whom God purposed to disciple.

How Paul Chose New Centres for People Movements

While Paul worked with that Greek-Hebrew Antioch community for a year, he must have come to know hundreds of relatives of Christians and to hear of thousands more. Some of these relatives from Cyprus, Pisidia, Iconium, Lystra and Derbe had quite possibly come to Antioch during Paul's year there and had joined in his hours of instruction. According to the record some of the Christians who had first spoken of the faith to Greeks in Antioch had come from Cyprus. They probably belonged to families who had connections on both the island and the mainland. Having won their relatives in Antioch, it was natural for them to think of winning their unconverted relatives, Jews and Greeks, in Cyprus.

If we think of the Christians in Antioch as having brothers and sisters, mothers and fathers, uncles and aunts, in-laws, cousins and other kinsmen in many of the towns of Cyprus and Asia Minor we shall begin to see the probable outreach of the new Christians through their own family connections. Some Jewish woman in Antioch may have said to Paul: "I have a brother in Iconium. He has for many years longed for the coming of Messiah. How I wish it were possible for him to hear you. He has a large house and has prospered in business. He would give you a genuine welcome. Do let me send him word?" Or some Greek Christian might say: "Our firm has business in a town called Lystra. My second cousin on my mother's side lives there. He and his family regularly attend the synagogue. He is coming to Antioch in a few days. He is a man of great influence. If he were to be convinced, he would insist on your going to Lystra." If we postulate 300 Christians in Antioch, and the likelihood is that there were many more, their relatives would be numbered by the thousands and would be scattered all over that part of the world. It is to us an inescapable inference that Paul at Antioch must have known of many such relatives and must have realized their enormous importance in the extension of the faith.

It may be deduced that every group brought in greatly multiplied the numbers of those relatives who were intensely interested. Every new synagogue which was reached by Paul yielded him a considerable number of men and women who, fired by his incandescent faith, would naturally talk to him about their relatives in as yet unreached towns and cities. Thus he would come to know of scores of communities in which the Gospel would be heartily welcomed.

The last chapter of the book of Romans yields a deep insight into this advance information possessed by Paul the missionary. He had never been to Rome,[1] but he had half a dozen relatives there and knew by name at least twenty-six people. Of these Priscilla and Aquila had worked with him in Corinth, pursuing their trade and fanning the flames of the Christian movement. Then there was Epœnetus, the first convert in Asia. Mary and Persis were also in Rome. They had "worked hard for the Lord". Was this before their marriage, in Corinth or Jerusalem? Had they been members of Paul's congregation in Antioch? We do not know. But Paul knew them well. Andronicus and Junias and Herodion were actual kinsmen of Paul's. Two of them had been in prison with him some time and were men of note among the Apostles. They had been Christians, prob-

---

[1] We are aware that many scholars believe that this chapter is not part of the original letter. But the main reason for this belief is only a supposition that he could not have known so many persons in Rome before living there. This begs the question, and takes no cognizance of the mobile mercantile Jewish population on the one hand, and of the intricate web of relationships so well known by Paul on the other.

ably in Palestine, before Paul himself had been baptized. There was a "beloved Stachys" and an Appelles "approved by the Lord". There was Rufus "eminent in the Lord" and Tryphena and Tryphosa "workers in in the Lord". We can only speculate on the connections which enabled Paul to know so much about these fellow Christians. We do know that Paul's own mother, or someone who had been like a mother to him, lived at Rome. It is reasonable to suppose that what Paul knew about Rome and recorded in a letter written before he got there, was also, possibly in lesser degree, a part of the advance information which he had about many other towns and cities.

Consider his experience at Philippi where there seems to have been no regular synagogue. Here only some women turned up at the place of prayer. Paul's party contained only men. Yet Lydia and her household were baptized immediately on hearing the Word, and she then said: "If you have judged me to be faithful to the Lord, come and stay at my house". How could Paul and his companions, all strange men, win so speedily the confidence of this respectable woman? Was Lydia simply overcome by the spiritual power which manifested itself through Paul? There is a much more reasonable conjecture. It is this. Either Lydia or some other woman there present knew Paul or one of his party, or else what he said about his friends made it clear to these women that they were dealing with genuine Jews—members of the family, so to speak. Without such credentials it is highly unlikely that Lydia would have immediately accepted these total strangers into her home and their unlikely message into her heart.

We are bound to infer that Paul chose and visited those centres where his advance information, purified by prayer and guided by the Holy Spirit, led him to believe that a church could be planted. It is quite likely that he inquired carefully whether a town were as ripe as it seemed to be. He largely chose centres where there were segments of the Jewish people predisposed to accept the Christian faith. He seems to have turned away from areas where, as far as he could foresee, folk were not likely to obey the Lord.

The New Testament shows no record of any attempt by Paul or other missionaries to Christianize, let us say, the district around Tarsus, and to hang on there for a hundred years whether successful or not. On the contrary, going to relatives and kinsmen, to those who could and did become Christians, was the habitual procedure. It is not claimed, of course, that Paul consciously built his programme around a sociological principle or that he determined to speak of Christ to none save those who had aunts or uncles in the Christian fold! But the general tendency here set forth is clearly visible in the records. Paul found himself in a vigorous seething People Movement and his was the most natural way in which to work.

It would completely misinterpret the record to imagine that Paul alone was responsible for the growth of the churches. On the contrary, Paul is simply the greatest among a host of witnesses all moving within the bond of relationship to bring their kinsmen to Christian faith. Apollos, Priscilla, Andronicus, Rufus and Mary are among those workers in the Lord whose names we know. Then there are both the humble refugees who went everywhere among their relatives "preaching the Word" and the nameless disciples who started the churches at Antioch and Rome. Finally, there were those through whose witness Paul found Jews who were anxious for him to prove to their fellows that Jesus was the Messiah. Without this People Movement we have Paul of the silent years. With it we have Paul the great missionary.

Let us consider in the light of People Movements Paul's desire to go to Spain (Rom. xv. 26). It is commonly said that he wanted to go there because it was an untouched country. There is not a word in Scripture to support this guess which seems to arise from missionary thinking of the last two centuries. Since there were Jews in Spain before Christ, it is much more reasonable to assume that he had contacts there. The field—the strictly limited field of the Jewish community and its Gentile connections—was ready for harvest and Paul longed to go to Spain.

How then did Paul choose fields of labour? To be accurate we must say that *he did not choose fields. He followed up groups of people who had living relations in the People Movement to Christ.*

Paul's Responsive Groups were Bridges

Those who thus had relatives in the early churches were doubtless aware of the Christian movement and of Christ as the expected Messiah. Through letters and messengers and the ordinary interchange of business and travel, the Christian faith cast its long shadow before it. When Paul arrived, he found the Jewish community anxious to hear him and to know all about this new Messiah. When he went to a synagogue he was invited to speak. Then he was invited to speak again. What happened in Pisidia (Acts xiii. 14f.) is typical of events where there were as yet no organized Christian groups. On the Sabbath Paul and his companions went to the synagogue. After the reading of the law and the prophets the rulers of the synagogue asked him to speak to the congregation. Paul then tells them that God has, by raising Jesus from the dead, made Him Messiah, and that through His name sins are forgiven and people are freed from what they could not be freed from by the law of Moses. The first messages of Paul were clearly messages for the Jews. He was striving to convince them that Jesus was the Messiah whom the Jews had been expecting, and to bring them into His glorious redeeming fellowship. Paul was busy expanding the already large and powerful People Movement to Christ and deepening its understanding of its Lord.

But Paul also intended to achieve the conversion of the Gentiles to Christianity. So after his first messages had achieved their purpose and many were convinced, and "Jews and devout converts" followed him home, he then taught of the universality of Messiah and of His availability by faith to men of all races. This message was tremendously appealing both to a section of the Jews and to the Greek proselytes and their uncircumcised relatives. For on the succeeding Sabbath "almost the whole city gathered together to hear the Word of God". This message was also tremendously irritating to a section of the Jews and they "were filled with jealousy and contradicted what was spoken by Paul".

As far as Gentiles were concerned, his messages appealed mainly if not solely to those "on the bridge". The synagogue community was composed of Jews of the Hebrew race, Jews of the Greek race, and a fringe of believing but uncircumcised Greeks. It was thus a bridge into the Gentile community which Paul recognized and used. His message brought conviction to those on "the bridge". Had he not used it his proclamation of the universal Christ might have left the Gentiles cold and untouched. Indeed, Paul before he came to Antioch may have been preaching this very Gospel in Arabia and Cilicia to Gentiles not on the "bridge". He may have told them of "the power of God for salvation to everyone who has faith, to the Jew first and also to the Greek. For in it the righteousness of God is revealed through faith." And because these Gentiles were not in living contact with believers, the message may have left them untouched. We do not affirm this dogmatically but, in addition to being the only reasonable conjecture as to what Paul was doing during the silent years, this lack of conversions is exactly what happens to-day all over the world as the Christian faith is proclaimed to non-Christians not in organic connection with believers.

Let us turn, however, to what we do know about the New Testament churches. This is that the Gentiles who were justified by faith were at the beginning mainly those who had been prepared through their Jewish contacts to receive the Gospel gladly. The New Testament bristles with examples of Gentiles prepared by Judaism. For example, there was a class of people found on the fringes of most synagogue communities. It was made up of Jews who had taken husbands or wives from other peoples. The Jews were permitted to marry only amongst themselves. Like every living people, they had effective social sanctions against taking women from or giving women to other peoples. Yet some Jewish women fell in love with Gentile men, and some Jewish men did the same with Gentile women. Such couples, unless the Gentile became a convert, were out of grace in the Jewish synagogue. Lois the Hebrew had a daughter Eunice. Both were good women. But Eunice fell in love with a Greek man who refused to become a Jew. Eunice lived with him and bore him a son Timothy. She continued to be a good devout woman with "a sincere faith", but was under the discipline and displeasure of the Jewish community. Timothy's father did not let him become a Jew. The message of Paul, that there was full free salvation for the Gentiles without their joining the Jewish race, must have come like food to this socially and spiritually hungry family group. There must have been many such family groups—convinced of the rightness of the Jewish

D

religious teaching yet excluded by its racialism. There were Gentile servants in Jewish homes, and Gentile patients of Jewish physicians, and Gentile officers under the influence of Jewish teachers, and many many others. Each one was a small bridge into the Gentile community. Paul sought to bring them all into the existing Christian movement which started out by being Jewish and ended up with the conversion of the Roman world. But at the outset he preached Christ mainly to a limited group of Gentiles, those Gentiles who were predisposed to become Christian by their Jewish contacts.[1]

The story of Palestine and of Antioch repeats itself. By means of "the Gentiles on the bridge" there came to be in town after town *within a comparatively short time a considerable number of Gentile converts who remained in close organic connection with large numbers of unconverted relatives.* These new churches, which had in them now large numbers of Greeks, were immersed in a Greek *milieu*, and a People Movement among the Greeks was under way. Thus in New Testament times were People Movements carried across race lines.

As we search for light as to how *peoples* become Christian, the story of the early Church has a great contribution to make. We see there the mighty People Movement which swept through Palestine. We see there an unplanned overflow into the Greek population at Antioch. Perhaps most important of all, we see how the

---

[1] If we except his defence before Felix and Agrippa and his brief exhortation to the crowd at Lystra, the book of Acts tells of only one occasion on which Paul deliberately preached to unattached Gentiles—his address at the Areopagus—and it does not seem to have carried conviction nor to have created a church. In none of the three or four instances of his converting unattached Gentiles as a result of a miracle do we read of these converts becoming influential in the Christian movement. A man as full of Christ as Paul was did, no doubt, speak to many outside the orbit of the Synagogue Community—*but the churches seem to have arisen uniformly inside these orbits.*

intentional missionary labours of the early Church, headed by Paul, were devoted in large measure deliberately to following responsive peoples and to expanding existing impulses to Christ in the hearts of peoples. On all counts the picture is one full of meaning for the present missionary movement.

IV

DOWN THROUGH THE CENTURIES

Has the discipling of peoples throughout the centuries followed the New Testament pattern? What occurred in the Roman Empire? Has the discipling of the clans in Scotland, the tribes in Germany, the various Slav peoples, the Irish and the Scandinavians, been characterized by the coming to Christian faith of peoples or of individuals? Has the Church grown by movements into the Christian religion of groups, villages, countrysides and whole kingdoms?

The Conversion of the Roman Empire

In the providence of God, the early churches spread far and wide through the Jewish People Movement to Christ. As the Good News was carried over bridges to the Gentiles two types of growth resulted.

Firstly, in many places the Church grew in the cosmopolitan melting pots in which many peoples lived close together. Marriages often took place across the divisions between peoples. The vivid consciousness of people-hood was replaced by the sense of being a part of the civilized Graeco-Roman world. The great urban centres such as Alexandria, Corinth, Antioch and Rome knew this breakdown of tribal feelings well before the times of Paul. The conversions to Judaism witness to this. In the churches of the urban centres the type of growth somewhat resembled that of the Protestant churches during the last hundred years in the West.

Large numbers of individuals were taken in one by one on the confession of their belief in Jesus Christ.

The Churches naturally urged that Christians marry within the membership of the Church. Converts from different peoples were now one new creation in Christ Jesus. They often arranged marriages among their sons and daughters. Thus remaining walls of partition were gradually broken down. The Christian Church was aiding mightily in the unification of all the Roman congeries of peoples. People Movements do not mean Churches permanently divided by caste-consciousness. They start keenly conscious of their racial heritage. They must start that way. In peoples without Christ, full of natural pride and caste-consciousness, how else could they start? But, as Christ rules in the hearts of His disciples and the effulgence of His glory fills His Churches, racial divisions are destroyed and peoples are unified. "For He is our peace, who made both one and broke down the middle wall of partition."

The early Churches in the Roman Empire manifested a strong tendency to swing from group ingathering to individual accessions. A catechumenate was developed in which there was a rigid course of instruction and discipline prior to baptism. Induction into the Churches was often individual and sometimes so secret that a man would not know that his own brother had become a Christian. In cosmopolitan areas, where a breakdown of the older people-consciousness had taken place, well-established churches seem to have been able to provide that home and consciousness of kindred which are so necessary before individuals from many peoples can, in a continuing stream, become Christians one by one.

Secondly, in some places the People Movements of the earliest churches found bridges to strictly endogamous peoples. In each such case the Christian movement there became largely a one-people Church. For example, the churches in the country districts south of Alexandria were probably composed in large measure of Egyptians. One thinks also of the churches of Abyssinia and Armenia, of Gaul and Dalmatia. The cities were cosmopolitan. The rural areas remained race conscious. Whatever growth there was in country districts can probably be put down to group ingathering.

Thus the rapid expansion of the Christian faith during the first four centuries witnessed both growth through individual conversions and a series of People Movements. The first type happened where people-consciousness had become dim, the second where it remained vivid.

The People Movements of Northern Europe

Vast sweeps of history can be easily over-simplified. Yet it may safely be said that, as a rule, the peoples of northern Europe came to the Christian faith in group movements, or in socio-religious movements, or in politico-religious movements. First one tribe would be discipled and then some years or centuries later another tribe would find a Christward movement being born within it. The story is too well known to need recapitulation. We merely call attention to it. *Christendom arose out of People Movements.* The only continent where most of the population became even nominally Christian was the continent which was won for Christ in a long series of People Movements!

The discipling did not, of course, mean perfecting. It meant the elimination of rival religious loyalties. It meant the abandonment of the authoritative gods of the old polytheistic faiths and the enthroning of the Lord Jesus Christ. The procedure by which Europe became Christian is often bewailed. Originally, it is said, to be a Christian meant something ethical. A

Christian was a spiritual person, seeking the things which are above, forgiving enemies, renouncing the works of the flesh, and manifesting the fruits of the Spirit. After Constantine, and particularly after these rough tribal conversions, Christians were little better than baptized heathen, and the Christian faith had more affinity with the worship of Thor than with that of the Prince of Peace. How much better it would have been, runs the argument, for the Church to have been discriminating, to have maintained an ethical standard and required those accepting baptism to conform to the law of love, or to have baptized only those individuals who gave proof of spiritual rebirth. Needless to say, those who so argue either are speaking ignorantly out of the ease and safety of modern western civilization or are thinking in terms of that extreme individualism which marks the Christian churches of the West after the industrial revolution.

Some reflection will show that a people always has its own pre-Christian religion around which the life of its members revolves. Individual conversions out of a people involve a terrific uprooting. In group conversions the individuals do not lose their social life in changing their religion. They need followers, they need leaders, they need wives, husbands, protection against their enemies, and the comforting association of folk of their own sort. The People Movement to Christ preserves these, while giving the entire community a new centre in the living Christ.

We can regret the Dark Ages which prevented the Christian churches from achieving greater perfection. But the choice was never between tribal conversions considered as a fourth-rate method of discipling and individual conversions considered as a first-rate one. It was tribal conversions or nothing. Had tribal conversions not been allowed by the Christian churches there might well have been very little Christianization at all, and our Christian leaders of to-day might be leading war dances around the Sacred Oak.

The Social Factors in the Reformation

The more modern religious movements growing out of the Reformation show even more plainly the social nature of religious change. Luther, Calvin and Knox were not content to expound a purified faith and then to let all who wished to enter do so one by one. To begin with, the power of the Roman church would not have permitted this. If the right were to triumph, as these Christian reformers saw the right, it must have power enough to overcome the power of Rome and thus to open the door to a purified Christianity. That meant that whole communities, dukedoms, kingdoms, princes with their armies, must be brought into the Protestant fold. History does not indicate that any large body of illiterate folk made a conscious and intelligent choice between Roman Catholicism and Lutheranism, or between Anglicanism and Presbyterianism. Their leaders made the choice, partly on religious, and partly on political grounds, and the population followed their leaders. We, who are inheritors of the evangelical faith, living in a day when universal education and the stress on the rights of the individual are so common as to be accepted as unquestionable, need to remember that the masses of our own ancestors not so very long ago simply were not equipped to make intelligent individual decisions independently of their leaders. Our right to individual choice was gained for us by the mass transfer of loyalties by our forebears. The vast majority simply followed their leaders. We shall have to concede that mass transfer of loyalties did, as a matter of historical fact, open the door for a more vigorous and a more spiritual understanding of the Christian faith.

We ask whether the discipling of peoples through the centuries has followed the pattern which we first saw in the New Testament. We get a definite affirmative answer as far as the initial discipling of nothern Europe and many later changes of allegiance are concerned.

V

THE CHARACTERISTIC PATTERN OF THE GREAT CENTURY

Dr Latourette has given the name "the Great Century" to the time between 1800 and 1914. He says: "When consideration is given to the difficulties which faced it, in the nineteenth century, Christianity made amazing progress all around the world. It came to the end of the period on a rapidly ascending curve. Its influence on culture was out of all proportion to its numerical strength. It had an outstanding role as a pioneer in new types of education, in movements for the relief and prevention of human suffering and in disseminating ideas."

How did Christianization proceed during the Great Century? This is a most important question because most of our present thinking is coloured by the missionary effort of this century. When we think of missions today, we think of those with which we are familiar, and which prevailed in China, Africa, India and other countries during the Great Century. Since this century produced a radically new and different approach, the older kind of missions which existed for 1,800 years have tended to be forgotten. The missionary and the churches tend to think that the only kind of missions and the only kind of Christianization possible is that used with greater or lesser effect during the past 150 years. The Great Century created a new method to meet a new situation. Both situation and method are worthy of our closest study.

The New Situation Described: The Gulf of Separation

Missions were carried on from the ruling, wealthy, literate, modern countries, which were experiencing all the benefits of political and religious freedom, an expanding production, and universal education. In the year 1500 European visitors to India and China described countries which compared favourably with their own. But by the nineteenth century the West had progressed while the East had stood still, so that there was a great gap between them. Western missionaries went to poor, illiterate, medieval and agricultural countries. The gap widened with the passage of the years, for the progress of the West continued to be greater than that of the East. While it is true that missionaries tried to identify themselves with the people, they were never able to rid themselves of the inevitable separateness which the great progress of their home lands had imposed upon them.

This gulf became very clear in the living arrangements which European and American missionaries found necessary. Their standard of living at home was many times higher than that of the average citizen on the mission fields, though it could not compare with that of the few wealthy Chinese, Japanese and Indians. Modern medicine was unknown. Health demanded big bungalows on large sites. Servants were cheap and saved much domestic labour. The people of the land generally walked, but the missionary was accustomed to a conveyance and so he used one. The colour of his skin also set him apart. He could not melt into the generality of the inhabitants of the land as Paul could. He was a white man, a member of the ruling race. To this day in the rural sections of India, seven years after independence, the white missionary is frequently addressed as *Sarkar* (Government). The missionary was an easy victim not only to malaria but to intestinal diseases. He had to be careful about what he ate. The Western style of cooking agreed with him, whereas the Eastern style did not. So in matters of food also there came to be a great gulf between him and the people of the land.

There were practically no bridges across this gulf. There was nothing even remotely similar to the Jewish bridge over which Christianity marched into the Gentile world. Staggering numbers of people lived on the fertile plains of Asia, but not one of them had any Christian relatives! Even in the port cities there were none. *Mésalliances* between white soldiery, rulers or commercial people and the women of the various lands were so resented on the one hand and despised on the other that they served as barriers rather than bridges. The normal flow of the Christian religion simply could not take place. Separated by colour, standard of living, prestige, literacy, mode of travel, place of residence, and many other factors, the missionary was, indeed, isolated from those to whom he brought the message of salvation.

The missionaries did indeed learn the languages of the country and learned them well. They served the people with love, taught their children, visited in their homes, went with them through famines and epidemics, ate with them, bought from them and sold to them, and, more than any other group of white men in the tropics, were at one with them. Thus, it will be said, this emphasis on the separateness of the missionary is exaggerated. To the student of the growth and spread of religions, however, it is apparent that these casual contacts described above are just that—casual contacts. They are not the living contacts, the contacts of tribe and race and blood, which enable the non-Christian to say, as he hears a Christian speak: "This messenger of the Christian religion is one of my own family, my own

People, one of us." Casual contacts may win a few individuals to a new faith, but unless these individuals are able to start a living movement within their own society, it does not start at all.

The separateness we describe seemed likely to last a long time. It existed in an unchanging world, where the dominance of the West and the dependence of the East seemed to be permanent. Missionaries thought, "There will be centuries before us, and, in a 400-year relationship like that of Rome to her dependent peoples, we shall gradually bring these peoples also into the Christian faith."

This grave separateness faced Christian missions during the Great Century. When the churches and their missionaries have no relations, no contacts and no bridges over inter-racial gulfs, what do they do? How do they carry out the command of their Lord? When there is no living approach, how do they go about the Christianization of peoples?

The New Method Evolved: The Exploratory Mission-Station Approach

If there is any aspect that is typical of modern missions, it is the mission station with its gathered colony. Missionaries facing the gulf of separation built mission stations and gathered colonies of Christians.

They acquired a piece of land, often with great difficulty. They built residences suitable for white men. Then they added churches, schools, quarters in which to house helpers, hospitals, leprosy homes, orphanages and printing establishments. The mission station was usually at some centre of communication. From it extensive tours were made into the surrounding countryside. It was home to the missionary staff and all the activities of the mission took place around the station.

Together with building the station, the missionaries

gathered converts. It was exceedingly difficult for those hearing the Good News for the first time, knowing nothing of Christians, or of Christianity save that it was the religion of the invading white men, to accept the Christian religion. Those who did so were usually forced out of their own homes by fierce ostracism. They came to live at the mission colony, where they were usually employed. Orphans were sheltered. Slaves were bought and freed. Women were rescued. Some healed patients became Christian. Many of these usually came to live at the mission station. They were taught various means of earning a livelihood and directed into various forms of service. They formed the gathered colony.

This kind of mission approach took shape out of the individualistic background typical of much Protestantism in the eighteenth and nineteenth centuries. To be a Christian was to come out and be separate. For converts to leave father and mother invested their decisions with a particular validity. To gather a compound full of Christians out of a non-Christian population seemed a good way to proceed. Frequently it was also the only possible way. The universal suspicion and often the violent hostility with which Christianity was regarded would have forced into the gathered colony pattern even those who consciously sought integration. This, then, was the pattern which was characteristic of most beginnings in the Great Century. We call it the exploratory mission station approach, but from the point of view of the result of mission activity, it was the exploratory gathered colony approach.

It was excellent strategy in its day. It was a probe to ascertain which peoples were ready to become Christian. Christianity must be seen to be stable before it will be accepted as a way of salvation. Peoples are not going to commit their destinies to a faith which is here to-day and gone to-morrow. Men must see over a period of years what the Christian life means and what Christ does to persons and to groups. While the Good News is first being presented and the Christian life demonstrated the mission station and the gathered colony are essential. As we look back over the last hundred years it seems both necessary and desirable for there to have been this approach. With all its limitations, it was the best strategy for the era. This approach has been no mistake. It fitted the age which produced it. It was inevitable.

The Road Branches According to Response

This beginning, adopted by practically all missions, may be considered as a road running along a flat and somewhat desolate plain and then dividing, one branch to continue along the plain, the other to climb the green fertile hills. Whether missions continued on the flat accustomed road (of the gathered colony approach) or ascended the high road by means of the People Movement Approach depended on the response given to the Christian message by the population and on the missionaries' understanding of that response.

Where the number of conversions remained small decade after decade, there the mission remained the dominant partner and the Mission Station Approach continued and, indeed, was strengthened. It was strengthened because the gathered colony furnished Christian workers so that the mission could expand mission healing, mission teaching and mission preaching. Where the number of conversions mounted steadily with every passing decade till scores of thousands were Christian, there the Church became the dominant partner and the mission turned up the hill road. It started using the People Movement Approach.

These two roads, these two ways of carrying on mission work, are distinct and different. Clear thinking

about missions must make a sharp differentiation between them. Each must be described separately. The
People Movements, the hill road, will be described in
the next chapter. The remainder of this chapter will be
devoted to describing the widening road on the plain,
the way in which the exploratory phase gradually
turned into the permanent Mission Station Approach
or gathered colony approach.

Small response was not expected by the early missionaries. The exploratory Mission Station Approach
was not launched as an accommodation to a hard-
hearted and irresponsive population. It was regarded as
a first stage after which great ingathering would occur. Even
after the Basel Mission had lost eight of its first ten
missionaries in nine years, the heroic Andreas Riis
wrote back from the Gold Coast in Africa, "Let us press
on. All Africa must be won for Christ. Though a
thousand missionaries die, send more." The exploratory
gathered colony approach was adopted with the expectation that the Christian faith would sweep non-
Christian lands bringing them untold blessings.

But these expectations were often frustrated by
meagre response. In the light of the event Professor
Latourette can now serenely write:

> The advanced cultures and faiths of Asia and North
> Africa did not yield so readily as did those of the primitive
> folk, either to Western civilization or to Christianity.
> This was to be expected. It has usually been character-
> istic of advanced cultures and their religions that they
> have been much slower to disintegrate before an invading
> civilization.

But the meagre response was not expected by the
early messengers of the Church. It was disappointing.

A factor in the small response, whose importance cannot be overestimated, is that, partly because of the indi-

vidualistic bias of the missionaries and partly because of the resistance of the hearers, conversions were mainly *out* of the tribe, *out* of the caste and, indeed, *out* of the nation. Converts felt that they were joining not merely a new religion, but an entirely foreign way of living—proclaimed by foreigners, led by foreigners and ruled by foreigners. Converts came alone. Often even their wives refused to come with them. Naturally conversions were few. A vicious circle was established: the few becoming Christian one by one set such a pattern that it was difficult for a Christward movement to be started, and by the lack of a movement converts continued to come one by one and in very small numbers. In many parts of the field it was as psychologically difficult for a person to become a Christian as it would be for a white man in South Africa to join a Negro Church knowing that his children would intermarry with the black children. The person not only became a Christian, but he was generally believed to have "joined another race". When, among peoples which intermarry only amongst themselves, a man becomes a Christian, his old mother is likely to reproach him, saying, "Now whom will your sons marry? They cannot get wives from amongst us any more."

The Exploratory Approach Becomes Permanent: Terms Defined

Where meagre response continued, there gathered colony missions gradually accommodated themselves to carrying on mission work among populations which would not obey the call of God. Once this occurred we may say that the mission, which had started its road-building on the plain, with the intention of reaching high fertile land as soon as possible, settled down to road-building on the barren plain as its God-given duty. It found plenty of good work to do. It never admitted, even to itself, that it had really given up hope of

E

reaching the hills; but that is what had actually happened.

In order to understand what occurred we shall define three stages in mission work:

Stage I. The mission sets out on the desolate plain with the intention of taking to the hills as soon as possible. This is the exploratory Mission Station Approach.

Stage II. The mission continues on the desolate plain, and has concluded that it is impossible to mount to the hills. This is the permanent or ordinary Mission Station Approach, which we know to-day. It is equally truly called the gathered colony approach. We shall use both terms interchangeably.

Stage III. The mission takes the road branching off to the fertile hills. This is described in the next chapter and is the People Movement Approach.

Let us now see how Stage I grew into Stage II.

Diversion to Secondary Aims

As a result of the small response, gathered colony missions were easily diverted to secondary aims. Sometimes when a famine occurred the mission cared for thousands of orphans and became for the next twenty years in effect a vast orphanage. The evangelistic work was still called the central task, but the orphanages claimed the lion's share of the budget. Around the orphanages were built great institutions. Missionaries, permanently located, were the heads of the orphanages. Since they commonly lived at the centres they had an influential voice in mission policy. It was expected that the orphanages would provide indigenous preachers for the proclamation of the Gospel. When it became apparent that the people of the land were not espousing Christianity in any but the smallest numbers, the institutional work appeared as more solid, more tangible, more rewarding. The church that thus grew up was at least there; it was visible. If people were not becoming Christians, what matter; a great work was being done, and the foundations were being firmly laid for a mighty church which would start growing some time in the future. Indeed, the solid nature of a church based on famine orphans and one-by-one converts, as opposed to that built on a group movement out of an illiterate people, became a matter of considerable pride, and leaders consciously turned from seeking "large numbers of ignorant converts".

Sometimes the mission was pressed into educational work. The leading men of the vicinity begged the mission to start a school. The children of the small Christian community needed a school. The Bible could be taught every day to every pupil. Many of the pupils came from the best homes of the city. The missionary was splendidly equipped to teach English—who could teach it better? To know English was a burning desire in the hearts of many youths. Prestige accompanied school-work but the schools rarely led to conversions. An occasional exception merely proved the rule. But there was no question of the liberalizing effect of mission schools. Boys who had gone through mission school and college usually had a deep respect for the Christian faith and the Lord Jesus Christ. They saw that the Christian movement was a good thing for the country. The ethical message of Jesus was readily absorbed. Leading men sent their sons to Christian schools, "because we like the type of character they develop there". In short, the indirect effects of mission schools in terms of the betterment of non-Christian nations were large. Considerable numbers of missionaries and, in some cases, entire missions, meeting meagre success in the discipling of peoples, turned to institutional work. This offered, not a rapidly growing Church, not a body of saved persons, but something which looked like the first steps toward a later widespread adoption of the Christian faith. The non-Christian faiths were being re-formed, the intense opposition to Christian work was being lessened, and numbers of secret believers were, it was hoped, being increased.

Missionaries in charge of schools often worked with cultured students who, in later life occupying posts of influence, expressed in gracious terms the debt they owed to Christian missions. They often rendered some notable service to the Christian cause. Leaders trained in such schools often led the district or the nation into great social advances. It was difficult not to compare the results of school work with the results of evangelistic work to the definite detriment of the latter. Even in the rare cases where the mission had succeeded in starting a Christian movement these illiterate rural Christians contrasted unfavourably with the products of the in-direct approach through schools.

Sometimes the diversion to secondary aims came through medicine. A mission dispensary was opened partly to relieve the suffering people, partly to break down prejudice and partly to witness to the message. The demand was unlimited. People would pay highly for treatment. The volume of work grew by leaps and bounds. So did the income of the hospital. The training of nurses, doctors, technicians and compounders was added. Large institutions grew up which dwarfed those of any other mission enterprise. One, two, and three, missionaries were assigned to those medical centres, which were defended in terms of their indirect effects. How could Christian leaders, having at their disposal means for the relief of suffering, fail to be compassion-ate? Did not this great ministry of healing bear its own silent witness to the Great Physician? Furthermore, the hospital enterprise, using mostly Christians as staff members, training mostly Christians, was giving to the gathered colony a tremendous opportunity for profitable and honourable employment.

We can appreciate highly all these results and support vigorously such a medical enterprise, and at the same time note that it did not give birth to any Christward movements of peoples. Indeed, the largest, most famous missionary medical centres seem to have grown up where there are no great growing churches. Where great populations have not turned to Christ, there are great hospitals; and where great populations have turned to Christ, there are few great hospitals.

Thus the Mission Station Approach, frustrated by meagre response, turned to secondary aims.

Mission Work Comes to be the Goal

Not only did missions turn to secondary aims but they came to consider them primary. Orphanages, schools, hospitals and agricultural enterprises were developed. Generations of missionaries devoted their entire lives to them. They found their consolation and satisfaction in the service of the non-Christian nations, the general alleviation of ignorance and suffering, the creation of a friendly attitude toward the mission, if not toward Christianity, and the rich service of a small Christian community. They hoped that at some time all these would work together for the Christianization of the land in which they laboured. The gathered colony became essential to the expansion of the mission. The missionaries and their national colleagues knew no other type of mission work. What they were doing *was* mission work, and was the finest kind of mission work! This was Christian missions at their best! Were such Christian leaders to be asked to evaluate their tasks in terms of the Christianization of peoples, they would quite likely reply that they were not interested in an increase of mere numbers, or that what they were doing was Christianization of the finest sort, or that the missionary enterprise has its various branches and that the Christianizers were doubtless Christianizing and the educators were educating!

The sending boards and churches made no distinction between mission enterprises serving the primary aim and those serving these secondary aims. All were equally valuable mission work. Indeed, the need of promotion among the sending Churches turned all into "grand works". Any kind of an enterprise could usually be carried on by a missionary, from teaching non-Christians how to grow peanuts to discipling a caste or tribe and, provided it was carried on with verve and vigour, it would be enthusiastically backed by the home base. Able missionaries came, inherited situations, "splendid pieces of mission work", poured their own enthusiasm and life into them, enlarged them, called for and sometimes obtained more missionaries and more money for them, and, in turn, passed on the torch to others. Whether anything was added to the discipling of peoples was an entirely different matter and one to which neither the missionary nor the mission, nor the home boards, nor the churches paid much attention.

This is scarcely the atmosphere in which Christward movements of peoples can originate. Both on the basis of *a priori* possibility and historic fact, we may affirm that once a mission station comes to be an institutional centre its chances of starting a Christward march of any of the peoples in its area are small. Pickett, in his monumental study,[1] noted that what we call

---

[1] *Christian Mass Movements in India*, J. W. Pickett; *Christ's Way to India's Heart*, J. W. Pickett; *The Mass Movement Survey of Mid-India*, Pickett, Singh and McGavran. These are obtainable from the Lucknow Publishing Company, Lucknow, U.P., India, and are essential books for those concerned with mission strategy.

People Movements often start many miles away from mission stations. The staff of the typical mission station do not look for a growing movement, and probably would not have time to spare for it were one to come and sit on their doorstep asking for spiritual nurture. Such typical institutionalized Mission Station Approach actually prevents the start of Christward movements. It may be claimed that it is preparing the ground for Christianization in the future but it is certainly not fathering any People Movements now.

The Churches Born of the Mission Station Approach

The first aim of missions is the establishment of churches. So, as we start to examine the results of the Mission Station Approach we turn to an inspection of the kind of churches which mission stations have fathered. These we shall call Mission Station churches or gathered colony churches.

They have some favourable characteristics. They are composed of greatly transformed individuals. The membership is literate. They come to church with hymn-books. They can read their Bibles. There are many among them who are specially trained beyond the ordinary school. In some stations there are many high school and college graduates on the church rolls. The membership contains a goodly proportion of day labourers and artisans, household helps and casual labourers, as well as teachers, preachers, medical workers, clerks, and other white-collar workers. In some places factory and railway employees form a considerable part of the membership. On the whole the Mission Station Churches are made up of people who are soundly Christian. There is not much superstition among them and not much temptation to revert to the old non-Christian faiths. The membership is proud of being Christian, and feels that it has gained tremendously by belonging to the Christian fellowship. There are, of course, many nominal Christians and some whose conduct brings shame on the church. But even these are likely to send their children to Sunday School and church!

They are organized into strong congregations. They have good permanent church buildings on land indubitably theirs. The pastors and ministers are usually qualified people. The services of worship are held regularly. The elders, deacons and other elected members form church councils and govern the church. The giving would probably compare favourably in regard to percentage of income with that in the Western churches, though often most of it is provided by those in mission employ. In some churches the giving is exemplary and there are many tithers. All told, the impression is that of small, tight, well-knit communities, buttressed by intermarriage and considering themselves to be a part of world Christianity.

On the debit side, these mission station churches are lacking in the qualities needed for growth and multiplication. They are, in truth, gathered churches, made up of individual converts, or "brands snatched from the burning", or famine orphans, or a mixture of all three. The individual converts and rescued persons have usually been disowned by their non-Christian relatives. The famine orphans have no close connection with loving brothers and sisters and uncles and aunts. Furthermore, the lives of these Christians have been so changed, and they find such satisfaction in the fellowship of their own sort (i.e. other mission station Christians) that they feel immeasurably superior to their own unconverted relatives. This is particularly true when they come from the oppressed classes. The second generation of Christians is even farther removed from their non-Christian relatives than the first, while in the third generation, in the very land where they live, the gathered church members know as a rule no non-Christian relatives at all. The precious linkages which each original member had as he came from non-Christian society and which are so needed for reproduction are all gone. A *new people* has been established which intermarries only within itself and thinks of itself as a separate community.

The Christians of the gathered colony approach have a vivid realization of the power of education. It has been education, they feel, that has lifted them out of the depths. They are keen for their children to receive as much education as possible. They skimp and scrape that their boys and girls may go on to school and proceed as far as possible on the road to a B.A. or an M.A. But they do not always have a vivid experience of the power of God. Many would grant that it was Christian education which had lifted them—an education given to them in the name of Jesus Christ. But on such experiences as the power of the Spirit, the forgiveness of sins and the blessedness of faith, many mission station Christians are likely to have a weak witness. "Become Christians and educate your children", they are likely to say. "It won't do you much good, but it will be wonderful for your sons and daughters."

The gathered colony churches usually have a vivid consciousness of the mission as their parent. The churches tend to feel that it is the business of the missionary to head up a wealthy social service agency, designed to serve the Christian community. It sometimes happens that the members of a mission station church, sensing the obvious fact that there is only limited employment in a mission station, look on new converts as a labour union would on immigrants. They draw the easy conclusion that if more people become Christians, the resources of the mission will be spread

thinner and there will be less for each of the existing
Christians. Cases have occurred where they have actu-
ally discouraged possible converts from becoming
Christian.

Gathered colony churches are often over-staffed.
They are too richly served by foreign missions. Their
members acquire a vested interest in the *status quo*. In
one typical mission station church of 700 souls we
find a missionary in charge of two primary schools and
one middle school for day pupils, another in charge of
a middle boarding school for girls, a missionary doctor
and his nurse wife who run a hospital, and an evangelistic missionary who gives half his time to the Christian
community. Then there is a national minister who is a
high school graduate with theological training, five
high school graduates who teach the older boys and
seven high school graduates who teach the older girls,
four evangelists, five Bible women and a primary school
staff of six. Missionaries, who, with less than half these
resources, are shepherding large numbers of Christians
who have come to Christ in some People Movement,
may gasp with unbelief that such heavy occupation
could occur. Yet both the national and the missionary
leaders of such mission station churches consider that
they really are managing with a minimum degree of
foreign aid!

The Missions Fashioned by the Mission Station Approach

We now turn toward the second result of this approach, namely the mission stations themselves. Any
visitor to the mission field is likely to come away with
the idea that mission work consists in schools, hospitals,
leper asylums, agricultural institutes, printing presses
and the mission compounds from which these multi-
farious activities are carried on. The churches would
seem to be a small part of the whole and subservient to

the mission station. This impression would be largely correct.

A characteristic of static mission stations is that they have an institutional life many times greater than is needed for the little congregation and quite impossible of support by it. The congregation is made up quite largely of the employees of the big mission institutions. The mission resources far exceed those of the church; and the mission personnel dwarfs the leadership of the church. Hence the work remains mission-centred even when devolution turns the management of churches, schools and hospitals over to nationals. It is quite possible to find a mission station where nine-tenths of the management is in the hands of the nationals, and where the church remains just as dwarfed as it was when foreigners were in charge. The institutionalized mission station is like an inverted pyramid, with huge accumulation of service organizations dominating the little congregation. This inevitably creates the idea that to be a Christian is to receive aid from institutions rather than to live a Spirit-filled life.

The mission station, from the point of view of the Christianization of a civilization and its Peoples, should be considered the *temporary* encampment of an army. If its houses and institutions must be sacrificed that the church may be planted, they should be considered expendable. But the psychology of the Mission Station Approach is never this. It is almost impossible for one who is immersed in the Mission Station Approach to avoid the conviction that his primary duty is to preserve the station where he works and to carry it forward to new heights of service and usefulness. Campaigns are waged "to save this historic station". The mission station becomes an end in itself, instead of a means to the discipling of peoples.

Growth comes hardly to the Mission Station wedded to a Gathered Colony

Any new work must be undertaken from money which "belongs" to the older work. Were the supporting Board, let us say, to send $10,000 additional budget to the field, that $10,000 would be regarded by every missionary and every national in the mission as belonging to the existing work. Were the proposal to be made that this sum be spent in some work which definitely planned for the creation of a People Movement, the proposal would seem to each person in charge, national or foreign, as an attack on his own budget.

The Mission Station Approach is also handicapped against growth because it has been so small in past decades, and it has been so necessary that work be carried on without using the growth of the church as a criterion of evaluation, that now most persons in charge honestly believe in patiently carrying on the work whether baptisms occur or not. "Mission work" comes to be the end rather than the "Discipling of Peoples". Most persons in charge, foreign or national, are in non-growing areas. The loyalty of the person in charge is naturally given to his work or station rather than to any seemingly impossible "Discipling of Peoples". Committees, made up of those who have poured out their lives for the work in their stations, tend to revolve around the pulls of various established works, all of them, including the evangelistic efforts, unsuccessful in discipling peoples. The missionary family, which nowadays includes many nationals, knows intimately the few thousand Christians who make up the church which the mission has fathered and mothered. These few Christians and their children become the supreme concern of the missionary family. It is easy for the leaders of the mission stations to think that their reason for existing is to help this small static church to become more literate, more healthy, more wealthy and more godly, whether Christward marches in surrounding peoples are induced or not.

A mission administrator was once faced with the fact that in one section of his field a Christward movement among a certain people seemed about to begin. He wrote at once to the person in charge of that station saying: "A question which comes to my mind is whether we have the funds to make this movement possible. Certainly your small budget will not be adequate. Each one of the stations is pressing me for more funds to run the existing work. We might quietly squeeze a little out here and there, but you cannot count on much. The other stations simply will not stand for it. You cannot expect your work to prosper at their expense. You had better be careful that you do not start something larger than you can shepherd." Granted that such an attitude is unusual, that it can be found at all is eloquent testimony to the static nature of the Mission Station Approach. The entire missionary movement exists so that Christward movements among peoples may be begun and extended, so that "Peoples may be Discipled". Yet such is the nature of the common missionary approach of the last century that, when in the providence of God they occur, they must be carefully restricted to keep them from getting so big that they upset the nicely proportioned machine designed to bring them about!

For all these reasons such missions are not likely to start growing churches, no matter how much longer aid from the West is continued. From the point of view of fathering Christian revolutions in surrounding populations, the Mission Station Approach has serious and constitutional weaknesses.

The National Awakenings Caused by Missions

The third major result of the Mission Station Approach has been a national rebirth in those nations where missions have been at work. Part of the advance of Western culture in these lands has doubtless been due to the impact of Western rulers, to the fertilization of thought through books, but much can fairly be credited to the vast penetration by the missionary movement. Its stations were centres of education and healing. They were seed-beds of revolutionary Christian ideas about justice, brotherhood, service and the place of womanhood. We cannot estimate too highly the social dynamic of modern missions. We have seen how they turned to those forms of enterprise through which Christian ideas could be absorbed by the population without formal transference of allegiance to the Christian faith. In this they were highly successful. Had these nations turned to the Christian faith by conversion, the national awakening would have taken place on a far deeper and sounder basis. Still, even when they appropriated only the ideas produced by Christian civilization, they entered upon an era of progress and enlightenment the like of which the East has never seen.

In India the Christian doctrine of the Brotherhood of Man cut directly across the Hindu conception of caste. The beneficiaries of the Hindu religion, the High Castes, had from time immemorial held the inferior peoples, the Low Castes, in subjection. The brotherhood of the Christian religion, more than any other one factor, made it difficult for the High Castes to receive it. Yet as brotherhood was preached, practised and demonstrated, a change was forced upon Hindu thinking. The High Castes saw that when the lowest of the low, the Untouchables, became Christian and received an equal chance of education and culture, they became as good as the best that the High Castes could produce. High Caste belief in the reality of caste distinctions was shaken. When in this century large numbers from amongst the 60,000,000 Untouchables began to become Christian, then the High Castes began to fear that, unless Untouchability, and indeed all distinctions based on caste were removed, the Untouchables would move *en masse* into Christianity. In the constitution of the country the Low Castes have written guarantees of equality which bode well for the future of India. No more revolutionary measure could be imagined. Yet it has come to pass without bloodshed or tumult. It is an achievement of the past 150 years of Christian Missions in which the mission stations have played a notable part.

Fifty miles off the railway in one of the most backward provinces of India, where the ferment of Christian ideas could scarcely be expected to permeate, there stands a little temple at a place where water gushes to the surface of a vast plain and flows throughout the driest part of the year. The temple is ornamented with images protraying a male god in various poses copulating with his devotees. It is hundreds of years old and the images had never offended the religious sensibilities of the residents. But within ten years after a small Christian outpost had been established half a mile away the images were plastered over. To-day, twenty years after, they are being gradually replaced by images of the male god alone. The mission stations have exerted a reformatory influence on the religions with which they have been in contact. In the renaissance of the religions of the East, which is so prominent to-day, the stimulation and purification caused by the proximity of Christianity has had a determinative influence. There are some Christian leaders who doubt whether an artificial addition of ethics to a religion which throughout the centuries has not evolved its own, is desirable.

Desirable or not, the Mission Station Approach has achieved it in great measure.

The social revolution caused by modern Christian missions, unlike most revolutions, has been bloodless. Missions have not led war bands and have not forced social changes. Through the quiet and peaceful processes of love and service, the criticisms voiced to the rising generation in schools, the example set in unselfish labour, public opinion in favour of social advance has been created on a large scale. Christian missions have also caused change through the challenge of their successes. "Unless we reform our society," the leaders of the land have said, "all these people will become Christian."

This result of the Mission Station Approach has been well summed up by Latourette. He says of Christian missions:

> Few even of those most closely associated with them, realize fully their magnitude, their skilful adaptation to the conditions of the era which is now passing, their remarkable vitality and their enormous contributions to the race. They have been and still are one of the most amazing features of an amazing age. Whatever the mistakes made and the crudities displayed, and they have been many, none who have had an active share in the missionary movement need ever feel apologetic for the sum total of the results. They should only be humbly and profoundly grateful for the privilege of association with an enterprise which has made such notable contributions to the welfare of millions of men and women.

But—the Era is Drawing to a Close

However, as Latourette points out, the era is passing. The days in which the mission stations could exert a major influence on the affairs of Eastern nations are drawing to a close. The sleeping nations are now awake. At the headquarters of the provincial and national governments are whole departments, amply provided with millions of money raised by taxes, whose chief duty it is to plan for the future of the nations. The tens of thousands of students who journey to the West for education, the flood of publications in all the major languages of the land, the advent of the movie, the loudspeaker and programmes of social education, the sensitiveness to foreign criticism, the intense desire to prove their own nation the equal of any on earth, and the resentment felt at foreign leadership—all these presage the end of an era in which mission stations in the urban centres exerted an influence out of all proportion to their numbers.

Mission schools in Asia and North Africa no longer have the influence which they once had. In the beginning they were the only schools. But now they form a small percentage of the total, and are being crowded into the background. It is still true that there are a few outstanding Christian schools in most countries, mission schools, convent schools, which are known as the best in the land. Even so, they do not get 1 per cent of the students. There was a day when they had 50 per cent of the sons of the leading families. Mission educationists cannot dodge the plain fact that mission schools cannot expect to wield the influence which they did in the days when Western cultures were first arriving in Asia and Africa.

What is true of schools is also true of mission station hospitals. Up till 1945 the Central Provinces of India had not produced a single qualified doctor. Its university had no standard medical school. The only fully qualified doctors were a few immigrants from other provinces and missionary doctors from abroad. But to-day there are four hundred students in the medical college of its university. As this flood of physicians flows out over the cities and towns and eventually the

F

villages of this province, the present near monopoly of the Christian hospitals is likely to be destroyed. The same sort of thing is taking place in one awakened nation after another.

Non-Christian nations are impatient with foreign tutelage. They believe it is demeaning to their national pride to admit to the need for guidance from any Western nation. The East, particularly India, honestly believes that, except for mechanization and industrialization, the West has little to give to the "spiritual East". The excoriations heaped upon Western nations by their own prophets, crying out against race prejudice, economic injustice and recurrent wars, are taken at their face value by the nations of the East. The West comes to be looked upon as soul-less, materialistic, unjust, money-mad, and moved by none but ulterior motives. The temper of these days in the East is not that of humbly sitting at the feet of missionary tutors.

It would be giving a distorted impression if the last few paragraphs were to imply that Christian missions have no more usefulness as cultural "hands across the sea". In the days ahead when nations are forced into closer and closer co-operation, all friendly efforts to interpret nations to each other will be of value. The continued residence of Westerners in the East will doubtless do good. But the days of great secular influence of foreign mission stations apart from great national Churches are probably about over.

They should be over for a further reason: there is now a use for mission resources which will do more for nation building, more for international peace, and more for the Church than the further penetration of non-Christian faiths and cultures from the vantage point of a foreign mission station.

Salute and Farewell

So has run the characteristic pattern of the Great Century. An age of tremendous mission expansion in terms of geography and influence; an age of heroism and devotion and self-sacrifice; an age of the meeting of two cultures separated by a wide gulf which, through the mission stations, outposts of goodwill and faith, has slowly drawn closer to the point where one world is in sight; an age when there is hardly a race or nation in which there is not found the Church.

So has run its pattern. But that age is now over. A new age is upon us. A new pattern is demanded. A new pattern is at hand, which, while new, is as old as the Church itself. It is a God-designed pattern by which not ones but thousands will acknowledge Christ as Lord, and grow into full discipleship as people after people, clan after clan, tribe after tribe and community after community are claimed for and nurtured in the Christian faith.

VI

THE GOD-GIVEN PEOPLE MOVEMENTS

While the typical pattern of missionary activity has been that of the Mission Station Approach occasionally People Movements to Christ have resulted. These have not as a rule been sought by missionaries—though in Oceania, Indonesia and Africa there have been some exceptions. The movements are the outcome of the mysterious movement of the Spirit of God. Their pattern of growth is very different from that described in the last chapter. They have provided over 90 per cent of the growth of the newer churches throughout the world. The great bulk of the membership and of the congregations of the younger churches consist of converts and the descendants of converts won in People Movements.

In spite of this, we maintain that People Movements were the exception, and that the typical approach of the last century was the Mission Station Approach. The number of mission stations from which Christian movements have started is small compared with the number serving static churches. Mission enterprises are, for the most part, those which serve non-Christians and gathered colony churches. The leadership of many conferences on missions comes largely from those who know and are immersed in the Mission Station Approach. And, as Dr Hendrik Kraemer writes: "Missionary thinking and planning in this revolutionary period are still overwhelmingly influenced by the Mission Station Approach." The Mission Station Approach must then be taken as the typical outcome of the past years, and the People Movements as the exceptions.

In dividing mission work into these two varieties—that operating through the Mission Station Approach and that operating through the People Movements—it is recognized that there is some mission work which cannot be classified under either head. For example, there is the translation and printing of the Scriptures. We are not attempting an exhaustive classification, but a practical one into which more than 90 per cent of missionary activity can be placed.

Some People Movements Described

Adoniram Judson went to Burma as a missionary to the cultured Buddhist Burmese. But he took under his wing a rough character, by name Ko Tha Byu, a Karen by race. The Karens were among the backward tribes of Burma. They were animistic peasants and were supposed by the Burmese to be stupid inferior people. "You can teach a buffalo, but not a Karen," was the common verdict. Judson spent six months trying to teach this former criminal, now his servant, the meaning of the redemptive death of our Lord Jesus Christ, and made such little progress that he was inclined to take the common verdict as true. However, he persisted, and a few months later Ko Tha Byu became a convinced, if not a highly illuminated, Christian.

As Judson toured Burma, speaking to the Burmese of that land, Ko Tha Byu, the camp follower, spoke to the humble Karens in each vicinity. The Karens started becoming Christian. Here a band of ten families, there one of two, and yonder a jungle settlement of five families accepted the Lordship of Christ. We do not have the data to prove that those who came were inter-related, but it is highly probable that chains of families were coming in. A chain reaction was occurring. We can reasonably assume that among his close relatives alone, to say nothing of cousins and second cousins, Ko Tha Byu had a host of excellent living contacts. The early converts doubtless came from among these, and their relatives.

Judson, translating the Bible into Burmese, was concerned with more important matters than a Christian movement among a backward tribe. He never considered the Karen converts as more than a side issue. His later associates, however, the next generation of missionaries, included some who were veritable Pauls, expanding the movement as far along the paths and across the rice paddies as possible. To-day there is a mighty Christian Movement among the Karens and their related tribes in Burma, numbering hundreds of thousands of souls. The Christian Karens are the educated Karens and will provide the leadership for the mixed population of Karens, Kachins and other tribes which predominate in parts of Burma. The Christward Movement among the Karens may well be the source of a Church numbering millions, and exercising a decisive influence upon the history of all South-East Asia.

By contrast, the Mission Station Approach to the Buddhist Burmese has yielded its ordinary quota of small, static mission station churches with a membership of perhaps 20,000 souls for all Burma.

The Karen Christians are good Christians. In a hundred sections of Burma there are communities of Christian Karens with their own church building, their own pastor, their own tradition of regular worship, their own Sunday school, and a Christian tribal life which augurs well for the permanence of the Christian Churches of Burma. The Karens, discipled through a

People Movement, and now in the process of perfecting, are not under the delusion that a nominal Christianity is worth anything to God. The thousands of churches scattered across the country contain a normal proportion of earnest Spirit-filled Christians. They are "reborn Baptists" who will compare favourably with the reborn Baptists of any land.

We stress this because it is a mistake to assume that People Movement Christians, merely because they have come to the Christian faith in chains of families, must inevitably be nominal Christians. Such an assumption is usually based on prejudice, not fact. All churches face the problem of how to avoid creating nominal Christians. Even Western churches, made up of only those individual converts who testify to regeneration, soon come to have a second and third generation who easily grow up to be nominal Christians. The policies of the churches may vary in their ability to produce Christians vividly conscious of their own salvation. People Movements in themselves do not encourage the production of nominal Christians.

Up in the north of Pakistan there was a lowly people called Churas. They were the agricultural labourers in a mixed Muslim and Hindu civilization. They formed about 7 per cent of the total population, and were Untouchables. They were oppressed. They skinned dead cattle, cured the skins, collected the bones and sold them. They had been largely overlooked by the missionaries preaching Christ to the respectable members of the Hindu and Muslim communities, and organizing their few hard-won converts into mission station churches. Then a man named Ditt from among the Churas turned to Christ, continued to live among his people, despite their attempts at ostracism, and gradually brought his relatives to the Christian faith. The missionaries were at first dubious about admitting to

Christian fellowship these lowest of the low, lest the upper castes and the Muslims took offence and came to think of the Christian enterprise as an "untouchable" affair. But those who became Christians were pastored and taught and organized into churches. Because the converts came as groups without social dislocation the efforts of the pastors and the missionaries could be given largely to teaching and preaching. Attention did not have to be diverted to providing jobs and wives, houses and land for individual converts. The Mission to whom God had entrusted this Movement was made up of devout men and women and they gave themselves to the task. The outcome was that at the end of about eighty years there are no more Churas in that section of India. *They have all become Christians.*

Whereas the church in mission station areas often numbers no more than one-tenth of 1 per cent of the total population, in the Chura area *the church* numbers 7 per cent of the population. There are congregations in many of the villages and a Christian witness is maintained, not primarily by foreign missionaries, but by the citizens of Pakistan.

In Indonesia there is a large mission work. In addition to static gathered colonies there have been also a comparatively large number of God-given People Movements. In the north of Sumatra there is a flourishing Batak People Movement, numbering hundreds of thousands. In 1937, on the island of Nias, off the north-west coast of Sumatra, there were 102,000 Christians: in 1916 there were none. In the northern parts of the Celebes the Minahasa tribes were by 1940 fairly solidly Christian and in the centre the growth of People Movements was rapid. There were tribal movements toward Christ in the Moluccas, the Sangi and the Talaud Islands. Around the year 1930 between eight and ten thousand a year were being baptized in Dutch

New Guinea. In the 1920's on one of the islands not far from Timor several thousands were baptized as a result of a People Movement. By 1936 the number of Protestant Christians was reported to be 1,610,533. The Roman Church also has increased by numerous People Movements. In 1937 there were 570,974 members of the Roman Catholic Church.

The only instance in the entire world of a few thousand Muslims being won to Christ occurs in Indonesia, in the midst of these numerous People Movements. It is also interesting that in Indonesia there is apparently a bridge between the natives and the Chinese immigrants, a bridge over which Christianity can cross. If this were strengthened it might well happen that more Chinese would become Christian indirectly *via* the People Movements of Indonesia than have been won in China itself.

In Africa there have been a large number of People Movements. The day is not far off when most of Africa south of the Sahara will have been discipled.

There is an instructive case of People Movements in the Gold Coast. These have grown into a great Presbyterian Church. For nineteen years (1828–47) the Basel Mission of Switzerland battled to establish a foothold in the Gold Coast. Of the sixteen missionaries sent out ten died shortly after arrival. The daring expedient had to be adopted of bringing in eight West Indian families to demonstrate that black men could read the white man's Book, and to provide missionaries less susceptible to the ravages of the climate. During this time there had not been a single baptism. The first four baptisms were in 1847 among the Akim Abuakwa tribe. The following table shows how the Church grew.

Year	Church members	Year	Church members
1847	4	1894	12,000
1858	365	1918	24,000
1868	1,581	1932	57,000
1890	9,000	1953	137,000

Till about 1870 the records show evidence of the exploratory Mission Station Approach. Slaves were purchased, freed, and employed at the mission stations for instruction. Run-away slaves were given shelter. Labourers on mission buildings were settled on mission land. In 1868 there was one missionary for each thirty Christians. The Basel Mission had a gathered colony at each of its nine mission stations. But in the decade 1870 to 1880 outlying chains of families started becoming Christian, and several stations among the Tsui-speaking tribes began to be surrounded by small Christian groups in scattered villages. Schools were established in each and the groups gradually became churches. An important feature of this movement, like many other African People Movements, was that pagan parents frequently sent their children to Christian schools, desiring them to become Christians. The school thus had enormous influence.

Early growth was tribe-wise. Teacher-preachers, the slightly educated first generation Christian workers on whom so much of the discipling of the tribes of Africa has depended, were usually recruited from each tribe in which a Christian movement started. They were then trained and sent back to that tribe to teach others, shepherd the Christians and win others to Christ. Later, as Christian movements arose in practically all the tribes, they became a uniting factor in the life of the nation, and workers were appointed more or less regardless of tribal relationships.

The present 137,000 members are organized into

594 self-supporting congregations, led by seventy-two college and seminary trained African ministers, with over 500 unordained assistants. The church maintains a large system (95,000 pupils) of excellent parochial schools, which, because of government grants, cost the foreign mission little. Growth is continuing. In 1953 there were 13,000 baptisms.

Mission Stations and Church Headquarters

The towns and villages where missionaries assisting Christward movements live are called "Mission Stations". This is the universal terminology for centres of missionary activity. We should not be confused at this point. There are mission stations which are hemmed in, where the growth of the Church by conversions is exceedingly small. These are enmeshed in the gathered colony approach. Then there are the mission stations blessed with People Movements, where almost every activity of the station contributes to the conversion of chains of families. The mission station becomes the religious and cultural centre of a people. It has its schools, hospitals, seminaries and missionaries' residences. It will superficially look very like a static mission station wrapped up in its institutions and its small non-growing gathered church. But because it is serving a growing movement in a stratum of society, it constitutes a totally different kind of approach.

It would be helpful to missionary thinking if everyone, from the missionary societies of the sending countries to the church councils of the younger churches, would give two separate names to these two kinds of mission centres. Let the one continue to be called mission stations: let the other begin to be called church head-quarters.

The Churches Born of People Movements

The most obvious result of Christian missions which have been fathering and furthering Christward movements is a tremendous host of Christian churches. It has been calculated that there are well over a hundred thousand congregations of Christians brought to a knowledge of God through recent Christian People Movements. These exist in most of the non-Christian countries.

Let us consider the unexpectedly large number of People Movements. The Islands of the Pacific have been largely discipled by People Movements. India has its extensive list of movements from the Malas and Madigas, the Nagas and Garas, the Mahars and Bhils, and many others. Indonesia and Burma total well over a score of People Movements of some power. Africa has numerous tribes in which the churches are growing in tribe-wise fashion. Two new People Movements are being reported as this book is written: one in Formosa and one in Mexico. Our list might be made much larger. Each of these hundreds of People Movements is multiplying Christian congregations as it grows.

These scores of thousands of congregations have many features in common. There are many members of the churches who are illiterate. In some lands the percentage of illiteracy in the People Movement churches is over eighty. The pastors of the churches are usually men with about seven years of schooling plus some seminary training. The church buildings are often temporary adobe or wattle buildings, though there are many well-built churches among the older congregations. The foreign missionary cannot get around to see the Christians more than once or twice a year. He is usually a director of pastors, in reality a kind of bishop, carrying on the administration of the churches, while the actual leadership of the congregations is almost entirely in the hands of nationals. In some older People Movements to-day national ministers head the church, while missionaries work as assistants directed by the church council. The services to Christians, so marked in the Mission Station Approach, are very much curtailed. The numbers of children are so great that, aside from small unsatisfactory primary schools, few children get a chance at education. In the mission station churches it is common practice for every child to be sent, largely at mission expense, through school as far as his intelligence will allow him to go. But in the People Movement churches the bulk of the Christian population has available to it only such educational advantages as the average non-Christian shares. This makes for an illiterate and ignorant church membership.

In some African countries, the school picture is totally different. Government does its education through missions. In such lands the children of the Peoples Movements have excellent educational opportunities and the membership of the churches is growing up largely literate.

Scattered as the congregations are it is difficult to reach them with medical aid. Cholera and small-pox epidemics, sudden death from cerebral malaria, infant maladies which carry off children like flies, and health conditions which are a scandal to the human race, are characteristic of these myriad rural churches.

Yet People Movement Churches are remarkably stable. There are reversions, specially in the early days, but on the whole, once a people has become Christian, it stays Christian even in the face of vigorous persecution. In addition to the faith of each individual and the courage which comes from world-wide fellowship, the very bonds of relationship and social cohesion keep weak individuals from denying the faith.

The Missions Fashioned by People Movements

Missions serving People Movements are overburdened. On the whole they get about as much money per missionary as the static missions. Since the number of missionaries sent to the field bears no fixed relationship to the number of Christians in the indigenous churches, the big productive missions tend to have only about as many missionaries and hence as much budget as the big static missions. But since their responsibilities are so much greater, the People Movement Missions are unable to assist their churches as they should be helped.

One result of this is a good many arrested People Movements. Let us assume that a thousand persons have come to Christ in chains of families. Their shepherding takes all the funds that the mission station can use for such work, and a good deal more. To exploit the opening further would take so much additional effort that mission finances would be badly upset. This one station would then receive much more than was "fair" in relationship to other stations. So expansion ceases. Those who have come in absorb all the energies of the mission station and in about twenty years have become an educated Christian group which has no marriage connections with its former community. The Christward movement has become a large static mission station church or an "arrested" People Movement.

There is a beneficial aspect, however, to the chronic shortage of funds in growing church missions. There is no pampering of Christians. They early learn that discipling does not include getting them land, making them loans, giving them jobs and getting them out of scrapes. It is generally agreed that the less physical and financial support the missionary gives the indigenous Christians and congregations the better. When the mis-

sionary is short of money for the pressing enterprises of
the group movement, he is not likely to err in giving
financial aid to Christians in ways which are detrimental
to the growth of an independent spirit in the Church.

It is, however, regrettably true that People Movement Missions, facing a chronic lack of funds, come to
be content with a sub-minimum standard of achievement. If 85 per cent of the Church is illiterate—"Well,
that is just the way the Church is here." If only five
young men out of 15,000 Christians have gone to high
school in the last five years—"Well, this is really an
improvement upon the previous five years when none
went." If pastors as a rule are men of only a sixth-grade
education and a year of Bible training—"Well, it is not
good, but it is the best we can do with what the churches
raise and the mission gives." Many a People Movement
Mission has been short of funds for so long that it comes
to make a virtue of the necessity, to the great detriment
of the growth of the Church.

The mission station tendency to make the institution
an end in itself is also occasionally found at church
headquarters in the midst of a People Movement.
There are hospitals at the geographical centre of a
thriving caste movement which serve primarily non-
Christians. There are schools in cities at the centre of a
great rural church with only a very few students out of
the rural People Movement. The school finds its field
of work in educating the non-Christian boys of the city.
There are colleges in the midst of People Movement
Churches which can number on the fingers of both
hands all their graduates from among the growing
churches. Such institutions justify their existence in
typical Mission Station Approach fashion.

In Africa some church headquarters are in danger of
becoming station centred. Those heading up the large
central training schools get wrapped up in them. They

never work in the villages. They tend to form a station centred group and, in the business meetings of the church or mission, to vote as such. Whether the People Movement goes on growing or not becomes unimportant. Tensions develop between educational and evangelistic work. Africa has been relatively free of such tendencies, but the new educational and medical policies which governments are putting into practice build up bands of missionary specialists at the centres, thus making it easy to slip over into a Mission Station Approach.

In parts of Africa the church headquarters can be divided into those which serve arrested or completed People Movements, and those which serve growing ones. There is danger that men and money will be allotted, not on the basis of the growth of the churches, but on the familiar basis of "fairness to all stations". Thus in the midst of tremendous opportunities for discipling, a church headquarters serving an arrested movement of 10,000 souls might get just as much foreign assistance as one serving a greatly growing movement of 40,000.

Merely to be geographically connected with People Movements does not turn mission stations into church headquarters. Until those in charge of the institutions at the centres hold steadily in view that the service of the growing churches is the highest missionary service, there is likely to be a good deal of Mission Station Approach even in the midst of growing People Movements.

Unvalued Pearls

One of the curious facts about People Movements is that they have seldom been sought or desired. Pickett records, in *Christian Mass Movements in India*,[1] that most

[1] Abingdon Press, New York, 1933.

People Movements have actually been resisted by the leaders of the church and mission where they started. These leaders often had grave doubts whether it was right to take in groups of individuals, many of whom seemed to have little ascertainable personal faith. Nevertheless, despite a certain degree of repression, movements did occur. One wonders what would have happened had missions from the beginning of the "Great Century" been actively searching and praying for the coming of Christward marches by the various peoples making up the population of the world.

Those People Movements which did occur · were seldom really understood. The way of corporate decision was obscured by the Western preference for individual decision. The processes of perfecting the churches were confused with the process by which a people turns from idols to serve the living God. Even where there has been great growth, as in parts of Africa, faulty understanding of People Movements has resulted in much less than maximum growth and has caused needless damage to tribal life.

Christward movements of peoples are the supreme goal of missionary effort. Many who read this book will not agree with this, and, indeed, it has never been generally accepted. Yet we not only affirm it, but go further and claim that the vast stirrings of the Spirit which occur in People Movements are God-given. We dare not think of People Movements to Christ as merely social phenomena. True, we can account for some of the contributing factors which have brought them about; but there is so much that is mysterious and beyond anything we can ask or think, so much that is a product of religious faith, and so much evident working of divine Power, that we must confess that People Movements are gifts of God. It is as if in the fulness of time God gives to His servants the priceless beginning

G

of a People Movement. If that succeeds, the church is firmly planted. If it fails, the missionary forces are back to the preliminary stages of exploration. Yet the essential recognition that the People Movement to Christ is the supreme goal is not often made by Christian leaders. Gifts of God come and go unrecognized; while man-directed mission work is carried faithfully, doggedly forward.

It is time to recognize that when revival really begins in China, Japan, Africa, the Muslim world, and India, it will probably appear in the form of People Movements to Christ. This is the way in which evangelical Christianity spread in Roman Catholic Europe at the time of the Reformation. It is the best way for it to spread in any land.

Half-Starved to Death

Compared with the small compact gathered colony churches, in the People Movements there are always large numbers of Christians and congregations spread out across a countryside. This makes the task of spiritual nurture difficult. For example, I recently visited in Africa a church headquarters serving 150 congregations with a total of 30,000 souls. These congregations are scattered over an area of 100 by 200 miles. There is one missionary assigned to the supervision of the 150 churches and 100 church schools. With a motor truck he may get to see each congregation once a year. The congregations are grouped into three pastorates, each in charge of an ordained African, who has about fifty part-time catechists under him. Each ordained supervisor has a bicycle. His field averages forty by fifty miles in extent. He may get to see each congregation once in two months—if he is exceptionally vigorous. There are no women's workers. Most of the Christians are illiterate. Most congregations receive inadequate instruction and partake of communion irregularly. Nor do they engage in the worship of God at all sufficiently. Inevitably spiritual malnutrition on a large scale results.

Such People Movement Christians live at a low level. They are illiterate, ignorant, and superstitious. Their economic condition is probably poor. Compared with mission station Christians, they need more and better training. Though this is a larger and more rewarding task than mission station work, the church headquarters has no more money than the mission station. The churches it cares for are therefore chronically half starved.

There is a poignant tragedy in this chronic spiritual malnutrition. The impression is created that People Movement Christians, by virtue of their coming to Christian faith in chains of families, are necessarily Christians in name only. That People Movement churches contain many earnest Christians who really know and love their Lord, and that the ancestors of the modern missionaries came to Christ in sweeping politico-religious movements, are facts conveniently forgotten. The evidence actually seems to indicate that better Christians are produced as a result of "coming to Christ in chains of families" than by the method of "one-by-one out of a hostile environment"; and that spiritual starvation in any Church, whatever its cause, does certainly produce nominal Christians. It is a tragedy to ascribe the undesirable result to the only method by which the Church grows greatly.

Who starves the People Movements? Those who decide policies in modern missions are many. There are the missionaries themselves and their colleagues the national ministers. There are the bishops and supervisors of the churches. There are the ministers and supporters of the sending churches. Finally, there are the secretaries and officers of the mission boards. All these four groups of leaders are constantly weighing in their minds the relative values of various pieces of work. Consequently, it invariably happens that in the decision the mission stations are compared with the church headquarters. This is entirely right and proper. In the comparison, however, the growing churches frequently come off second best. Let us see why. The mission stations are easier to visit. They have been established at centres of transportation. A busy secretary in a two-months' visit can see more at a mission station in three days than he can of a growing church in a month. The persons in charge, national and missionary, also know their mission stations. They have been there frequently. They have not seen a tenth, and may be not 1 per cent of the unimpressive little village congregations. Then, too, the mission station churches seem to be so much more "Christian". They are so much more educated and orderly. Their members are persons of some influence in the towns and cities. Many of their members speak English, whereas practically all the country people speak neither English nor the standard vernacular, but only some dialect. The district missionary is constantly complaining about the low standard of his workers and the difficulties of adequately supervising them. No wonder the People Movement churches seem like "a difficult and somewhat unrewarding type of mission work" and thus are allocated resources which are much smaller than the number of their congregations would seem to require.

Thus growing churches are usually woefully under-manned, under-taught, under-cared-for and under-perfected. The speed of their expansion is slowed to a fraction of what it might be under maximum cultivation. Naturally, there have been exceptions to this generalization. There have been People Movements so compelling that no neglect could slow them down.

There have been missions which felt that the discipling of a given tribe or people was their high privilege and who bent every resource to that end. They realized that the success of their high schools and colleges was to be measured in terms of the numbers of new Christians from out the growing movement who passed through them; that the function of the medical programme was to make and keep a thousand congregations healthy; and that the primary duty of the mission was, by using every means possible, to develop the local movement into one which raced across the land to the geographical limits of the people within which it was thriving. But such competency has been the exception, not the rule.

Infant Mortality High Among People Movements

Partly because Christian missions have stressed secondary aims and individual conversions, partly because they have failed to understand how peoples accept the Lord Jesus Christ, and partly because the people concerned has resisted, there is a high mortality among new movements. The movement of a people is usually at the outset easily stopped. The numbers concerned are small and may remain small for a generation. The power available through numbers is extremely limited. The relationship with the foreign mission and the foreign missionary is difficult. It is easy to start wrong patterns with the little group of Christians. For example, when peasants become Christian and their creditors demand immediate repayment of loans secured by land, the missionary who loans money runs the grave danger of making evangelization seem a process of buying Christians, and if he does not loan money his new fellow Christians lose their precious land. If the children of the new churches are not educated at all, the movement may fail because the church is left illiterate. If they are highly educated, the second generation may move out of the villages into the cities and into white-collar jobs, and the movement may die out in the very places where it started. If the former leadership is recognized as the leadership of the new Christian churches there is danger that it will continue to lead the churches in sub-Christian practices or lead them back into paganism. If it is not recognized, it is likely that a contest for the people will develop between the younger and the older leaders. Any of these might prove fatal to the young movement.

Sometimes so much immediate ethical advance is required that the tender young movement dies. For example, sometimes the Christian leaders feel that the pagan society being discipled should, in the act of becoming Christian, abandon practices which many communities in the older churches still observe. But before baptism pagans do not have an ethical religion, do not have the Holy Spirit or the Bible and do not from childhood have the example and teaching of Christian leaders. To expect great measures of reform at the outset is putting the cart before the horse. Yet it is a natural error. Christianity should mean something spiritual. Conversion should be a great forward step. However, we would be well advised to bear in mind the simple orders which the early Church, facing this same problem, laid down in writing: "For it has seemed good to the Holy Spirit and to us to lay upon you no greater burden than these necessary things: that you abstain from what has been sacrificed to idols, and from murder, and from what is strangled, and from unchastity." To be sure, it is the part of wisdom to use the exaltation which accompanies any People Movement to secure what degree of social and spiritual advance can be achieved. But to lay on the newcomers such grievous burdens that they cannot even enter Christianity as groups is a serious error and one which has contributed to much infant mortality among new movements.

The nurture of new People Movements is difficult. There are very few persons who know how to rear them. The geographical difficulties are considerable, especially for missionaries unaccustomed to walking! The language barriers are serious because, though the intimate language of a people is likely to be some dialect, the Christian faith, its Bible, its prayers and its worship usually come to them in the standard language. The values cherished by the new converts are often curious even to the nationals from nearby movements or from the gathered churches. It is difficult for the first pastors, who have come from some other people, to know what is socially possible or impossible. These factors contribute to cauте the early demise of many new movements.

Five Great Advantages

People Movements have five considerable advantages. First, they have provided the Christian movement with permanent Christian churches rooted in the soil of hundreds of thousands of villages. For their continued economic life they are quite independent of Western missions. They are accustomed (unfortunately too accustomed) to a low degree of education. Yet their devotion has frequently been tested in the fires of persecution and found to be pure gold. They are here to stay. They are permanent comrades on the pilgrim way.

They have the advantage of being naturally indigenous. In the Mission Station Approach the convert is brought in as an individual to a pattern dominated by the foreigner. The foreigner has set the pace and the style, often to his own dismay. But such denationalization is a very minor affair in true People Movements.

In them the new Christians seldom see the missionary.
They are immersed in their own cultures. Their style of
clothing, of eating and of speaking continues almost un-
changed. Their churches are necessarily built like their
houses—and are as indigenous as anyone could wish.
They cannot sing or learn foreign tunes readily, so
local tunes are often used. Thus an indigenous quality,
highly sought and rarely found by leaders of the Mission Station Approach churches, is obtained without
effort by the People Movement churches. Church
headquarters, however, need to make special efforts to
keep thoroughly indigenous their training of People
Movement youth and leadership.

People Movements have a third major advantage.
With them "the spontaneous expansion of the Church"
is natural. The phrase "spontaneous expansion" sums
up the valuable contribution to missionary thinking
made by Roland Allen and the World Dominion Press.
It requires that new converts be formed into churches
which from the beginning are fully equipped with all
spiritual authority to multiply themselves without any
necessary reference to the foreign missionaries. These
might be helpful as advisers or assistants but should
never be necessary to the completeness of the church or
to its power of unlimited expansion. Spontaneous expansion involves a full trust in the Holy Spirit and a
recognition that the ecclesiastical traditions of the older
churches are not necessarily useful to the younger
churches arising out of the missions from the West. New
groups of converts are expected to multiply themselves
in the same way as did the new groups of converts who
were the early churches. Advocates of spontaneous expansion point out that foreign directed movements will
in the end lead to sterility and antagonism to their
sponsors, and that therefore the methods now being
pursued, here called the Mission Station Approach, will

never bring us within measurable distance of the evangelization of the world.[1]

Desirable as spontaneous expansion is, it is a difficult ideal for the Mission Station Approach churches to achieve. They might be freed from all bonds to the Western churches, they might be convinced that they had all the spiritual authority needed to multiply themselves, they might be filled with the Holy Spirit and abound in desire to win others to Christ, and yet—just because they form a separate people and have no organic linkages with any other neighbouring people—they would find it extremely difficult to form new churches. In People Movement churches, on the contrary, spontaneous expansion is natural. Both the desire to win their "own folk" and the opportunity to bear witness in unaffected intimate conversation are present to a high degree. There is abundant contact through which conviction can transmit itself. True, in People Movements this natural growth can be and, alas, sometimes has been, slowed down by the atmosphere and techniques of the all-pervading, gathered colony approach. But once these are recognized and renounced by the leaders of the People Movement churches, it becomes comparatively easy for spontaneous expansion to occur. Missions can then, like Paul, deliberately attempt to use the relatively unplanned expansion of a Christward People Movement to achieve still greater and more significant enlargement. Thus we come to the most marked advantage of these movements.

[1] The point of view developed in the following books is most important for any serious student of missions in the coming age. They are obtainable from World Dominion Press, London, and Friendship Press, New York: *Missionary Methods—St. Paul's or Ours?*, Roland Allen; *The Spontaneous Expansion of the Church*, Roland Allen; *Objective and Method in Christian Expansion*, Alexander McLeish.

Enormous Possibilities of Growth

These movements have enormous possibilities of growth. That these possibilities are to-day largely ignored and unrecognized even by the leadership of the churches does not diminish either the truth or the importance of this fact.

The group movements are fringed with exterior growing points among their own peoples. As Paul discovered, the Palestinian movement had growing points in many places outside that country. Just so, every Christward movement has many possibilities of growth on its fringes. For example, the Madigas have become Christians in large numbers. They are the labourers of South India. They have migrated to many places in India and even abroad. One cannot help wondering whether a fervent proclamation by a modern Madiga St. Paul carrying the news that "We Madigas are becoming Christian by tens of thousands each year: we have found the Saviour and have as a people come into possession of the unsearchable riches of Christ", might not start Madiga Movements in many parts of the world.

People Movements also have internal growing points; that is, the unconverted pockets left by any such sweeping movement. Here the leaders of the Christian forces must be alert to see to it that strategic doorways are entered *while they are open*. Doorways remain open for about one generation. Then they close to the ready flow of the Christian religion. Until the discipling of the entire people, there will be both internal and external growing points. Both will yield large returns if cultivated.

Of rarer occurrence are the bridges to other communities, such as that over which St. Paul launched his Gentile movements. In order to be called a bridge, the connection must be large enough to provide not merely for the baptism of individuals, but for the baptism of enough groups in a short enough time and a small enough area to create a People Movement in the other community. More of these bridges would be found if they were assiduously sought. More would be used for the expansion of the Christian faith if leaders could be led to understand them and become skilled in their use.

The possibilities for growth in People Movements are not by any means confined to developing new movements. Leaders of People Movement churches find that after the church has attained power and size the normal processes of growth, including the baptism of individual seekers on the fringes of the church, often produce more quiet regular ingatherings year after year than was the case during the period of the greatest exuberance of the movement. One might conclude that once a People Movement church has gained a hundred thousand converts, and the church has become indigenous to the land and forms a noticeable proportion of the population, it is likely to keep on growing. A moderate amount of missionary assistance, at places where the churches feel their need, produces results far beyond that which those accustomed to the mission station tradition would consider remotely possible.

Providing the Normal Pattern of Christianization

The fifth advantage is that these movements provide a sound pattern of becoming Christian. Being a Christian is seen to mean not change in standard of living made possible by foreign funds, but change in inner character made possible by the power of God. In well-nurtured People Movement Churches, it is seen to mean the regular worship of God, the regular hearing of the Bible, the giving to the church, the discipline of the congregation, the spiritual care exercised by the

Christian pastor, habits of prayer and personal devotion and the eradication of un-Christian types of behaviour. This life, centering in the village church, often built by the Christians themselves, is seen to be the main feature of the Christian religion. There are no impressive institutions to divert attention from the central fact. Christians become "people with churches, who worship God" rather than "people with hospitals who know medicine", or "people with schools who get good jobs". The health of the Christian movement requires that the normal pattern be well known, not merely to the non-Christian peoples, but to the leaders of church and mission and to the rank and file of members. The People Movement supplies the pattern which can be indefinitely reproduced. It is the pattern which has obtained throughout history, with minor variations.

Does the Method Replace the Message?

The historic message of the Christian Church has been: "Believe on the Lord Jesus Christ and you will be saved." The Church has good news for the world. It is that sinners by repentance and baptism in the name of Jesus Christ are saved by grace through faith. "God so loved the world that He sent His only begotten Son, that whosoever believeth on Him should not perish but have everlasting life."

Do we then maintain that we should abandon the message and turn to the induction of People Movements as the way of salvation? Are we proposing a method, when what is needed is more faith and more surrender to God's will?

Let us be clear on this at once. The method we advocate does not and cannot ever replace the message. God has a plan of salvation. This He has made clear in His Word. Only as men, individuals or peoples, accept it can they gain everlasting life. Jesus Christ is the same, yesterday, to-day and for ever. He is the revelation of God. There is no substitute for faith in Him.

Yet through all these twenty centuries the message has been presented in many ways. Some have been more successful than others in leading men to accept the Saviour. The way of group action is the one which has discipled most of the world. Through this method the message will be understood better, by more people, in a shorter time than by any other. The message is the Lord. His chariot is the People Movement.

The Power of God unto Salvation

Failure to win souls for Christ is commonly the cause of much heart searching on the part of church and mission leaders. "If only we were more spirit-filled, more constant in prayer, more holy in life, souls would be won and our church would grow", they say. Their theology stresses hot sparks. The heat of the spark, the degree of dedication, and the completeness of one's own salvation—these are the essential matters in the thinking of many. Radiant faith in the indwelling Lord is certainly essential. But the truth not often seen or stressed is that Christianity, like electricity, flows best where there is good contact. The power of God acts best within a people. We have seen in Chapter III how the power of God won a very large segment of the Hebrew people for Christ in the first forty years of the Church—and hardly touched the other peoples in the midst of which the Hebrews were immersed! It flowed with great power where it had good contact. St. Paul was a Spirit-filled man, a man of prayer, rich toward God, yet he made it his practice to go to those groups who had already been prepared by the decisions of their blood relations. This same phenomenon can often be observed down through the centuries. Christianity has flowed most powerfully when it has flowed within peoples. Electricity will flow through miles of copper wire, without jumping an inch to another nearby wire with which it is not in actual contact.

The president of a Christian college in a mission field once remarked to me that it was curious that those brought for baptism into the churches of the city where the college was, were often brought by the least reputable of the members of the churches. Investigation indicated that these people were the only Christians in living contact with their non-Christian relatives. The Christians in that city had come from the underprivileged strata of society. Rich service in a mission which stressed education had lifted most of the abler members of the church to a degree of culture and moral insight which put them out of touch with their relatives. Some of them actually disclaimed their relatives in an effort to improve their own social standing. The weakest members of the church were the only ones who had any real contact. It was through these contacts that sinners were being brought to Christ. There are many other illustrations of the fact that cold sparks with good contacts have, as a matter of historical fact, produced more growth than hot sparks with poor contacts.

Individual Salvation

Can salvation arise through a group decision? This is a most important question. Let us imagine a case in which, through a group movement, in some one year 500 have come to Christ. The leaders of the 500 have some real faith in Christ, some appreciation of His meaning for mankind, otherwise they would not lead their fellows out of "Egypt". But among the 500 there are probably scores whose becoming Christians means perhaps little more than being willing to go along with their friends. Does mere membership then in this

Christian group, without any more individual acceptance of Christ than is implied in a willingness to follow
the group into Christianity, confer salvation?

This difficulty in the fundamental theology of group
movement churches will loom particularly large to
those churches which practise believers' baptism, and
which broke with the older branches of Protestantism
over questions similar to this. Those who practise believers' baptism maintain that merely being born into
a Christian church and baptized into it in infancy does
not in any way confer salvation. They feel that neither
the baptism of infants who cannot believe, nor the
baptism of ignorant members of a group, has in it the
stuff out of which redemption is made.

But the difficulty also exists for those who practise
the baptism of infants. "It is one thing", they will say,
"to baptize an infant who is a member of a Christian
family and is exposed to the redemptive influence of life
in that family and in the church; and it is an entirely
different thing to baptize groups of persons out of
heathenism who cannot have the faintest idea what it is
all about."

This is to paint the difficulty in darker colours than
the facts warrant. Most groups being baptized have
received a great deal of instruction before baptism.
Very few come to the place of baptism without hearing
the Word of God many times. If 500 were baptized in
any one year, it would mean only forty persons a
month. A great deal of instruction can be given to each
one of forty persons in that time. In addition to this
instruction there is always a great awareness of the
Christian faith arising out of a multitude of experiences
over the decades before baptism. In most group movements there is the vital inner experience of having
observed other close relatives in the Christian faith, of
having watched them baptized and having heard their

pastor expound the Scriptures. So that there is considerable unformulated knowledge of Christ in the
minds of even the least active of the group.

Needless to say there is every reason for using the
one-by-one method, pressing the claims of Christ and
the meaning of discipleship on each individual within
the group. The more personal decision there is among the
members of a group the more it will please God and
the more blessing it will bring to itself. There is still
more to be said in defence of a genuine inner experience
for group movement converts. In the third chapter of
St. John it is recorded that: "This is the judgment, that
the light has come into the world, and men loved darkness rather than light." By "light" the writer clearly
means the Lord Jesus Christ, the Light of the World.
Every man is judged if he prefers darkness to light. The
light may be a faint glimmer or the noonday sun, but
whatever the degree of brightness, he is judged by
whether he follows it. The members of a pagan people
when that people first turns to Christ, may all reach
individual convictions that salvation is through Christ.
In some, although the degree of conviction may be
small, it is there. But it is to be borne in mind that the
capacity of most individuals in many societies for individual decision is small. Most decisions are shared
decisions. A wife is not taken or an ox bought without
consultation with others. For the group mind to be
formed, many individuals must express agreement. So
that we may truly say that *when a group comes to Christ,
every member has had a share in the final decision.* Only those
who have loved the light (even in a small degree) have
participated in the group decision. This truth is made
clearer by the realization that in most groups there is
(as was the case with the Jews in the first century) a
section that do not become Christian. Since each individual is free to move or to stay back, "coming with

others" indicates a degree of "following the light".

We believe, then, that in the initial discipling of a people participation in a group decision is a sufficient following of the light to confer salvation on each person participating in the decision. It is *not* "membership in the group" but "participation in following Christ" which is the vital factor.

Should We Be So Concerned with Mere Numbers?

Some people question any emphasis on numbers. They say: "Obviously the discipling of peoples is concerned with mere numbers. Those who are attracted by such a process fail to realize that even where a numerous church is not built up, precious souls are being saved. One soul is worth all our effort."

There are several answers to this objection. The first is that no numbers of redeemed persons are ever "mere numbers". Numbers of persons brought into living worshipping contact with the Way, the Truth and the Life are never mere digits. They are always persons beloved persons, persons for whom Christ died. They are our own brothers and sisters. As such the more who come to Christian faith the better. We consider any disparagement of "numbers" of converts ridiculous, and do not believe that on second thought many would advance the objection.

Then, again, evidence shows that qualitative advance is best made with socially whole men and women. People Movements toward Christ produce good Christians, better in many instances than the only other method being used. They are better, because Christianity means to them a way of life with Christ rather than a way of life with a rich foreign mission. They are better because they are less dependent on outside resources. They are better because they are more rooted in the soil, and more likely to continue living there. They are

H

better because, when well led, they worship God more regularly and give to God more of their substance. They are not as cultured in the Western manner as mission station Christians. They may not make as good an impression at first glance. But they are good Christians. We maintain that the discipling of *peoples* brings about more sound qualitative advance as well as much greater growth in numbers than the Mission Station Approach.

People Movements in nominally Christian Lands

Are People Movements the normal pattern of church growth in nominally Christian lands? Roman Catholics are carrying on a great missionary campaign in North America. Protestants are carrying out great missionary campaigns in Latin America. When Russian tyranny is softened or overthrown and freedom of conscience becomes a reality in the U.S.S.R., Orthodox, Protestants and Romans will seek to re-win to Christian allegiance those secularized by the totalitarian State. Can we say that People Movements are a normal pattern of such missionary labours in North America, Latin America, Asia and Russia?

In an individualized society, such as that of cosmopolitan and urban North America, the conversion of individuals is the principal form of church growth. But in large sections of Latin America, Russia and Asia, society still exists in a non-individualistic form. Wherever this is so, particularly where there are laws or customs which prohibit or prevent free intermarriage between Christians of the missionary church and the population being evangelized, *the missionary church must somehow or other start a People Movement, or it will be walled off and confined to an ineffective and expensive conversion of individuals here and there.* This is true because the gathered churches are "beach-heads" into the habitat of the human spirit, while the People Movement churches are "break-throughs" which open up race and nation to the beneficent liberating influences of the Good News.

VII

THE GATHERED COLONY STRATEGY IN THE LIGHT OF PEOPLE MOVEMENTS

The gathered colony or Mission Station Approach is to-day the universally accepted missionary method. Despite much talk, this basic procedure, inherited from the nineteenth century, is almost never questioned. It reigns supreme. It unconsciously dominates practically all missionary thinking. We do not lightly criticize its value, yet, since a strategy of missions which does not carefully test this bed-rock of modern missionary method is bound to be superficial, we must now ask: "In the light of the multitudinous People Movements what is the strategic value of the gathered colony approach to-day?"

This Approach is Seldom Seen in People Movement Context

We immediately face a strange fact. So compartmentalized are missionaries and mission stations that many of them know very little about any work other than their own. They do not see their own work in the light of the opportunities and responsibilities created by the People Movement. To use an illustration, the gathered colony missions are doggedly trying to build bridges at the particular places chosen by their earlier comrades. They are so absorbed in chiselling out blocks of granite that they have no time to carry the Christian message across the bridges which God has completed a few miles down the chasm.

I recently visited a mission station in India, established over a hundred years ago by an intrepid man of God. It is still vigorous. It has its babyfold, hospital and evangelistic work. The Christian community numbers 293. Of these about half are employed by or are financially dependent on the Mission. An annual expenditure of about $10,000 from the West is being incurred. I asked a senior evangelist if any of the neighbouring castes were responsive. He replied: "I have been preaching the Word for thirty years. In that time no one caste has yielded ten converts. What caste shall I say is responsive?"

These good friends have perhaps one chance in a thousand to initiate a Christward movement among some people in their district. But their resources, if carried across the bridge which exists not 200 miles away, would be the means under God of bringing a stream of Christian churches into being. Yet such is the outlook of the Mission Station Approach that there does not seem one chance in ten thousand that my friends will transfer their resources to the nurture of an actual growing church. They will not even take the pains to learn about the bridge. The presuppositions of the unquestioned Mission Station Approach blot out the light of People Movements.

Missions are Constantly Considered Homogeneous.

Because modern missions are wrapped up in mission work of many varieties, they see People Movements as but one kind of mission work. The missionary enterprise is therefore unable to recognize that when it deals with gathered colony churches and People Movements it is dealing with two different types of approach. The thinking and writing of missions make no distinction between these two situations. Speakers talk as if missions and the younger churches were homogeneous, the only distinction being that some were a little farther advanced than others.

A pertinent example of this failure to distinguish between these two types comes from the 1952 conference of the International Missionary Council at Willingen. This conference said: "Financial partnership between churches needs to be expressed primarily in sharing the burdens of missionary outreach, rather than in supporting the internal work of the Church." Willingen may have been pointing to the same opportunity which so engages our attention—that of the growing edge of the People Movement churches. But Willingen might equally easily mean that static gathered colony churches should have larger funds to proclaim the message to the unresponsive peoples in the midst of whom they live! And does Willingen mean that the People Movement churches, already neglected, are to have still less help in training their ministry and building up their own life? Why does Willingen speak thus vaguely? Could it be because the vital distinction between these two kinds of churches and missions was not clearly seen?

Hence Meaningless Diagnosis and Indiscriminate Support

The failure to recognize two different kinds of missions leads often to meaningless diagnosis. "Mission schools", writes an author of international fame, "have been built in such a style that the small church communities cannot even repair the buildings when the mission moves away. The church has been loaded with too much school." This stricture is largely true in regard to some churches—the gathered colony churches. But it is erroneous and misleading in regard to the great Christward movements where there are now not nearly enough schools, little or big. The Reverend Joel Lakra, head of the Lutheran Church of Chhota Nagpur, which numbers 200,000 members and receives very little money from the West, is the authority for the statement that this denomination has with its own resources built eleven high schools since 1941 (it formerly had one), and since 1947 has added about 500 primary schools (it formerly had about 500). A church like that could scarcely have had too many schools built for it by its mission. This stricture is also erroneous in regard to People Movement churches like those in Kenya where Government does most of its education through missions and pays for it. Here the large educational effort of the missions is of slight financial burden to either church or mission and has enormous influence in forming Christian character and sound churchmen. What is sorely needed is different names for these two types of churches and missions. How could physicians diagnose correctly if they were limited to the one word, "fever", in describing malaria, typhoid or polio? If this book makes "Gathered Colony Churches" and "People Movement Churches" household phrases in the thinking of missions, much will have been accomplished.

The lack of exact thinking in regard to the types of missions results also in indiscriminate support of all kinds of mission work. Under the present strategy, Christian leaders tend to think of missions as a conglomerate mass of mixed chicken-raising, evangelism, medicine, loving service, educational illumination and better farming, out of which, some time and somehow, a Christian civilization will arise! The treatment for all such splendid and self-sacrificing mission work is the same: pray for it and support it. Budget allocations are frequently made without due concern for the type of result being achieved. Enterprises which are actually discipling peoples and enterprises which are "quarrying the stone with which to build the piers, on which the bridge may later be built, over which discipling may sometime proceed" both receive equal valuation. Both are "fine mission work". Whether one or the other gets more or fewer missionaries and larger or smaller budgets will depend on various extraneous factors: the national importance of the field, the existing size of the work, the promotional appeal of the project, and the popularity and vigour of the missionaries involved.

However, much of this indiscriminate support depends on an unformulated belief that, since growth is impossible and all sorts of plans to serve the church are being tried, there is just one measure of the worth of a work: is it being faithfully and intelligently carried on? If it is, it deserves support. We would like to believe that if any Church or Mission, even those most deeply enmeshed in the gathered colony approach, were to become thoroughly convinced that the discipling of one of its own peoples was really under way, it would make the distinction called for, and assign priority to growing churches. Unfortunately, the beginning of a People Movement is not often easy to discern. It is likely to be thought of as a pet aberration of some leader. The way in which a movement starts, the groups of people who are baptized ("How do we know that these illiterates have been born again and really love the Lord?"), the slight degree of perfection in the beginning ("We are afraid that a scandalous moral laxity is permitted. No wonder the thing grows!"), the difficulty of shepherding ("I am not impressed with these baptized heathen, nor do I think we should encourage that sort of thing!") —all these combine to make those already committed to standard mission works dubious as to whether the movement is really a pearl of great price, and whether good established works should be cut back in order that this "experiment" may be developed. So, lacking assurance, the budget committee usually falls back on its regular routine and makes a "fair" appropriation to each enterprise.

The Crux of the Matter

But when the Mission Station Approach *is* seen in the light of People Movements, when the New Testament record is studied for light on how peoples become Christian, when the history of the Reformation is pondered and the mighty People Movement churches of to-day are visited, then it is clear that the gathered colony Mission Station Approach is a transient strategy designed to build bridges, but seldom succeeding. Failing to recognize the transient nature of the mission station and its gathered colony church, and erroneously considering it a permanent international Christian activity, the mission enterprise continues to put major emphasis on this outmoded approach. Though the conditions which necessitated the gathered colony approach have changed, the approach continues unquestioned. The missionary enterprise is using the strategy of an era now closing. It should switch to the strategy of the era now beginning. It has depended heavily on the mission. It should depend heavily on the church. It has built mission stations. It should now help build church headquarters.

A Final Question

Is there then any point of view from which the Mission Station Approach can be considered a good way to carry out the Great Commission? There is, we believe, only one.

Missions which feel called of God to carry the Gospel to completely unreached populations *hostile* to Christianity may still need to gather converts into a colony. This approach, somewhat modified, may be indicated where there are no indigenous churches at all. In such places mission stations would provide a place to stand on while the Gospel was being proclaimed. But from now on, in any gathered colony approach, deliberately adopted, there must be careful consideration of the relative weight given to exploratory work such as proclamation and philanthropy, on the one hand, and to the intentional development of People Movements on the other. The gathered colony must be recognized as a means to an end, to be discarded as soon as the end is achieved.

But with *friendly* populations it will be frequently possible to pass directly from proclamation to the formation of New Testament churches without going through the gathered colony phase. This will avoid the danger of getting stuck there. And if the myriads crying out to be discipled are to be reached in this generation, then all mission work must be rigorously related from the beginning to the growth of People Movement churches.

The approach to completely unreached peoples aside, some Christian leaders may answer this final question in the following fashion. "Yes," they will say, "the Mission Station Approach strategy is valuable. It fits our purpose exactly. To be sure, we are not primarily interested in the spread of the Church. We seek to bring about brotherhood, peace, enlightenment, and the gradual improvement of all religions and civilizations. We are here to do all the good we can, not to impose our faith on others." For those who wish to reinterpret Christian missions so that the ultimate aim is this kind of amelioration, the mission station is a possible instrument. However, this book is not written for those who so misinterpret Christian missions. What they propose is not Christianization through the Mission Station Approach strategy but Mission Station Approach Strategy as a substitute for Christianization.

There will be other friends who, as they answer the question, will say: "Certainly the present strategy is excellent. We believe that the growth of the Church is the goal of Christian missionary endeavour. We believe in the conversion of sinners. We believe that Christ wills the salvation of all these peoples in the midst of whom we live and work. But He is not limited to bringing converts in by socio-religious movements! He converted Paul and Sundar Singh and Kagawa and Sun Yat Sen as individuals. Under Mission Station Approach strategy we teach His truths, we preach His cross, we heal in His blessed name, we spread His Word. In His good time He will bring men and women and peoples and nations to discipleship. We are not to concern ourselves with the increase."

"Yes," we reply. "But when God, in His good time, does start bringing men and women in large numbers to salvation, *how will He do it?* What will be the pattern of their coming?"

To this our friends return: "Devout men and women, convicted of sin and knowing their Saviour, will accept baptism. They will form themselves into churches and start living holy lives. The difference between then and now will be quantitative. More people will come then. It will also be qualitative. The Church must come to have a far deeper and more Spirit-filled life. Only then will there be a spreading of the fire. We do not need methods or movements. We need robust faith. Given more holiness and more consecration to Christ, gathered colony strategy will cause the Church to grow greatly."

With deep sympathy for the religious feeling which lies back of such an opinion, and granting that God could work that way, we note that, except in melting pots and individualistic civilizations, God has not worked that way for 1,900 years and is not working that way to-day. God has been discipling the peoples. For every one out of a new people brought to Christian faith separate from his group, God has converted hundreds in chains of families. He has used the People Movement. That is the normal way in which the Christian churches have grown.

No, the second answer to our question turns out to be merely a restatement of the modern Western prejudice in favour of individual accessions. No matter how attractively stated, it is not a point of view from which the Mission Station Approach can be regarded as the best way to carry out the Great Commission during the coming era.

VIII

CO-OPERATING WITH GROWING CHURCHES
IS TO-DAY'S STRATEGY

The thesis of this book may now be fully stated. The era has come when Christian Missions should hold lightly all mission station work, which cannot be proved to nurture growing churches, and should support the Christward movements within Peoples as long as they continue to grow at the rate of 50 per cent per decade or more. This is to-day's strategy.

There are Now Enough Growing Churches

By "growing churches" we do not mean churches which are primarily recruited through the one-by-one process. As long as accessions from the non-Christians are one-by-one, from different levels in society, and result in no People Movement, any considerable growth will be rare and, even when achieved, temporary. Such a system can operate successfully only in a discipled society. By "growing churches" we mean organized cells of the movement of a people. Folk join these cells by conversion without social dislocation, without entering a new marriage market, and without a sense that "we are leaving and betraying our kindred".

Of this kind of caste-wise, tribe-wise, clan-wise or people-wise movements there are now enough *so that the entire resources of Christian Missions could be poured into them* and they would still be able to absorb more. If we revert to the analogy of the bridges across a gorge, separating a land of plenty from a land of scarcity, we may say that the building of approaches to future bridges by each mission station should now cease because there are *enough bridges already built to give access to most parts of the land of scarcity.*

All People Movements do not offer the same opportunity. There are large People Movements which have discipled the whole of one people and are now static, and there are those which have claimed for Christ only a third of their people and are growing at every point. There are those where part of the people has turned to Buddhism and part to Christianity and where the balance is unpredictable, and there are those in which the balance will almost certainly turn to Christ. There are vigorously growing movements and there are arrested ones. Of these latter some may be able to be revived, but some appear to be permanently stopped.

Support to each of these will be transferred in such amounts and by such means as will achieve ends which vary. For example, let us consider the Christward movement on some island which has brought to Christian faith all its residents. Should that unquestioned movement of a people be reinforced? The answer is probably "No", unless the inhabitants have marriage relationships with non-Christians on other islands. Those who have become Christian now have the Bible, the church, Christian leadership, and some connecting linkage with the world Church. Their reinforcement would not lead to an extension of the Christian faith. It would be better to permit this discipled people to pursue perfection through the efforts of their own churches under the guidance of the Holy Spirit, as an integral part of the world Church.

On the other hand, let us suppose a People Movement church of 200,000 souls. It exists in the midst of 700,000 as yet unconverted relatives and fellow clansmen. Discipling is proceeding at a satisfactory rate, seemingly held back only by lack of resources. Scores of places exist in which the Movement could be nurtured and extended. From the point of view of Christian strategy here would be a People Movement to the service and reinforcement of which the resources of many static mission stations could be transferred with immediate and dramatic results.

Within the far-flung Christian enterprise, there are many People Movements of a yet different character. They are the small, new and weak movements numbering a few thousand souls each. They can be stopped by many forces and arrested in their infancy. It would be easy to dominate them and serve them too well. Yet the present condition of many of them is that they suffer from excessive malnutrition and are on the verge of starvation. Here skilful and experienced reinforcement, of the right kind and of the right amount, is called for. Given this, gratifying growth may be expected.

Then there are the potentially fruitful situations, where some such picture as the following may be observed. There is a people which can be expected to welcome the Good News. A few score families, less than a 1,000 persons, have recently come in to the church. Among them there are natural leaders who are on fire to win their entire clan, caste or tribe for Christ. Such situations are not rare but they have been allowed too often to stagnate. Some have even been allowed to die. When they arise in the midst of the Mission Station Approach, they are exposed to all the hazards to which any secession is exposed and, in addition, suffer the evils of the Mission Station Approach pattern. But they are, nevertheless, points of real hope. If they were to be regarded as the *raison d'être* of missions and not as stepchildren, many of them could be reared to lusty manhood. They will require a degree of reinforcement and very skilful handling.

There is a special variety of potential People Movements in many parts of Africa where tribes of all sorts and sizes are leaving animism at a striking rate. They are going to accept something in the next thirty years: Catholicism, Protestantism, Islam or secularism. The faultiest missionary techniques used in this favourable environment will result in some parts of the tribes accepting the Christian faith. But, if full Christianization is to be achieved, vigorous discipling of peoples, the claiming of whole social units for Christ, must be pressed. Rapid discipling of entire tribes should be followed by an even more rapid production of an indigenous, self-supporting ministry. The high concentration of missionaries needed for the early stages can and should be sharply diminished once an African ministry has been trained.

Multiplying Growth by the Transfer of Resources

The missionary enterprise has not yet experienced the degree of growth which is possible. The magnitude of opportunities for church growth would be considered by most Christian leaders as beyond the bounds of possibility. Yet the world teems with unsuspected opportunity.

As concentration of resources on growing points comes to be the strategy of missions, we shall find ourselves in a new era of advance.

These resources may be sent to churches on the fringes of some movement where evangelism through the connections of the existing Christians may be expected to bring ingathering; or they may be used in aorgnizing the existing Christians all across the area for the purpose of reaching their relatives; or they may be sent to some new Cyprus, Macedonia or Rome, where groups of some responsive peopl<. are predisposed to become Christian. What possibilities open up before us as Christian missions become people-conscious, and Christward movements are intentionally followed throughout their geographical outreach. One example will suffice. There are Chinese churches in Hawaii, the Philippines, Indonesia, Formosa and Malaya, which might purposefully attempt a Pauline task: firstly, mightily to develop a People Movement amongst the Chinese of the dispersion; and secondly, to carry the Christian religion over their bridges to their folk in China—not to the Chinese in general, but to those strata of the Chinese with whom the churches of the dispersion are linked with marriage relationships.

In the shifting of emphasis from static to growing work, it is essential that the possibilities of growth be proved. There is too much at stake for missions to make major moves merely because the other pasture seems from a distance to be greener. It would be both tragic and wasteful for some mission in great faith to move much of its resources to the service of a People Movement, only to find that it was a permanently arrested movement. That is why only those movements which are growing at the rate of 50 per cent per decade or more should be considered growing churches. The normal increase by births over deaths is likely to provide a 15 per cent enlargement. This leaves a 35 per cent increase to be achieved by baptisms from amongst the non-Christian members of that people, for the decade as a whole. This in turn means about $3\frac{1}{2}$ per cent per annum for the movement. In a church of 1,000 persons that would mean only thirty-five accessions a year from among the non-Christians. A People Movement could scarcely grow less without being arrested. It should normally grow more. The norm of 50 per cent per decade is based on a study of the growth of these movements, and it is a workable figure which will serve meanwhile.

I

The healthy growth of People Movements will in some cases be helped by the nurture of the churches which compose them. Better spiritual nutrition would in some instances bring on more normal growth. In these cases church and mission leaders will wisely devote a part of the transferred resources to teaching a much larger proportion of their membership to read their Bibles, to sending more of their ablest youth through high school and college, and to training an informed, Bible-knowing lay and clerical leadership. But a danger to be avoided is that of giving rich service to the growing churches so that they come, like the older Mission Station Approach churches, to have a vested interest in foreign funds. It must always be emphasized that resources will be made available only as long as the movements grow.

Moreover, the impression should not get abroad that movements which are healthily independent, if a little gaunt, are to be flooded with foreign money. This would do untold damage. From the beginning it should be clear that any additional resources will not lessen the giving of the churches, and that any such lessening would automatically mean a reduction in foreign aid. The ways in which the new support is used must increase the self-respect and independence of the People Movement churches.

Strategic Peoples Receive Priority

A study of the prospects of growth shows that among the Christward movements of the world there are distinct differences in strategic importance. Some movements are keys to many peoples, some to an entire nation. Some seem to have little importance or linkage beyond themselves. Some peoples are important because they can be won now, and probably not later, or only by much greater effort. As the missionary movement embraces a mobile policy of discipling peoples, the strategic value of each people assumes great importance. It has, therefore, to be asked:

From the point of view of the greatest possible extension of Christianity during the foreseeable future, which growing churches should receive priority?

That this question is not yet being asked is indication enough that missionary thinking and planning, even in this revolutionary period, are still overwhelmingly influenced by the gathered colony approach.

There are several illustrations of this. Firstly, there is the Hump country: eastern Assam, northern Burma, northern Siam and north-west Indo-China. This is a land of forests, mountains and isolated valleys occupied by vigorous animistic Sinic tribes. The Hump country is a natural barrier between India and China, but potentially a bridge. It has ample rainfall and tremendous water power. There are few more strategically placed countries in the world. Its isolation is certain to disappear soon. The western fringe of its people has become Christian in Assam, where some districts are 80 per cent Christian. The southern fringe has become Christian in Burma and the eastern fringe in Indo-China. Perhaps a tenth of the total population has become Christian. The other nine-tenths are going to emerge out of their animism during the next fifty years into Buddhism, Hinduism, Communism or Christianity. The educated leadership of this congeries of peoples is overwhelmingly Christian. The Hump country would seem to have a strategic importance of the highest order. Were the indigenous churches on the periphery to have resources placed at their disposal they could very well guarantee that the Hump country will be a largely Christian country in the heart of Asia.

Secondly, consider the strategic importance of that strip of Africa where Islam confronts animism. There are sections of it which are strategically more important than others, but the entire area is of enormous significance. Its tribes will not remain animists. If they emerge into the Christian faith, the southward advance of Islam will be permanently stopped. But if they should emerge into the Islamic faith, not only will they be lost to the Church, but Islam will have a wonderful foothold from which to extend into the as yet unconverted population to the south. The response to Christianity of some of these tribes has been very encouraging, but they are on the whole lightly occupied. The People Movements among them, too frequently, have to take their chances for support along with other less strategic People Movements and with the gathered colony approach stations of their missions. The massing of support behind these movements seems something which Christian missions should be doing *now*.

A third illustration is taken from India. In the high country of Chhota Nagpur about 500,000 people have become Christians, largely from the Uraon and Munda castes. There is a large Lutheran church and a large Roman Catholic church. The Lutheran church is autonomous and receives little assistance from the West. All through Chhota Nagpur there are cases of the Christian religion spilling over into some other castes. All around Chhota Nagpur there are large populations of unevangelized Uraons and Mundas and allied castes and tribes. If there ever was an instance of a Christward movement teeming with possibilities of growth, this is it. Yet the Lutherans of Chhota Nagpur are not taking advantage of a tenth of the opportunities which are theirs. Here is a church to whom aid should be sent. Its great extension would establish the Christian movement in India in a position of entirely new influence. In any order of priority, the People Movements of the Uraons and Mundas would rank high.

The assignment of such priorities and their imple-
mentation is a task for missionary statesmanship.

The decisions are epochal. Christian missions must
cease being an enterprise in which all kinds of activities
are ranked as about equal in importance. Christian
missions must become the kind of a job in which priorities are put into force. This statesmanship will need new
information. No one now knows, no one now can know,
what Movements should have priority. The facts, carefully ascertained, might well prove all the illustrations
given above to rank low in order of precedence. But the
true facts can be ascertained once the cause of missions
is dedicated to massing support behind People Movements.

Why Move in the Face of Signs of Hope?

Some may ask: "Why move? There are plenty of
signs of growth here in this so-called static station. The
population has never been so friendly. We are over-
whelmed with invitations to come and proclaim the
Word. Ingathering seems just around the corner. To
move now would be folly."

We give thanks to God for the perennial hopefulness
of Christian leaders in mission lands. Without the com-
fort of hope the task in a static station would be drear
indeed. Yet there is a great distance between friendliness and baptism. Friendliness to a cheery foreign missionary or national agent is one thing. Readiness to
accept the Lord Jesus Christ as Saviour, to leave old
gods, to join a new religion, to be bitterly misunder-
stood by one's neighbours and many of one's relatives—
that is an entirely different thing. The one does not
necessarily lead to the other. Friendliness does not
gradually develop to the place where baptisms begin.
The only test whether a mission station is facing a period
of growth is a simple one: are men accepting baptism

there? Really, the question should be asked in a more definitive way: are groups of people, all of the same stratum of society and most of them inter-related, becoming Christians in their ancestral homes? Are they staying on there following their ancestral occupations and enduring what persecution may arise? Are new groups from amongst their relatives actively interested? Are they in turn being baptized? If the answers are in the affirmative, then there is no need for the static mission to move. It has the pearl of great price. But if the questions cannot be answered affirmatively then we must conclude that the signs of hope will not lead to ingathering, and that the mission should transfer resources.

Furthermore, most of those who plead that the present location is just as good as one in connection with a growing movement, while looking forward to their mission and their church beginning to grow, do not realize how such ingathering will come about. It is so far away in the future, and there has been such a complete lack of it in the past, that they have no idea as to the nature and form of church growth. One is left to conjecture that they expect such growth to be a normal continuation of their mission station set-up.

Shall We Leave in Darkness Those Who Have Never Heard?

This question rises naturally. "Are we as a brotherhood going to abandon the difficult fields? Do we not have Christ's command to preach the Gospel to the entire world—whether they hear or whether they don't? The Good News must be preached as a witness to all men."

In answering it we must remember three facts. Firstly, missions in the midst of irresponsive peoples show an uncontrollable tendency to veer away from proclamation and become missions of education, medi-

cine, social service and the general assistance of a
gathered church community. So that to think of our
static missions as flaming evangels is somewhat erroneous. Missions steadily confronted with closed doors
usually change the nature of their undertaking and
successfully defend the change to their supporters and
to themselves. Secondly, the time when the entire non-
Christian world was an untouched field and missions
had of necessity to be exploratory has now passed. The
Christian churches of the world are faced with many
areas where peoples are seeking Christ and are accepting Him in baptism, and with many where neither individuals nor peoples are seeking Him. If we had resources enough to develop both, then only would we be
justified in channelling resources into sterile fields.
Since we have limited resources, surely we must work
amongst those who can be won now. Thirdly and con-
clusively, the surest way to reach the unreached, now
after a hundred and fifty years of missions has given us
People Movements in large numbers, is not by main-
taining foreign missions, outposts of foreigners in the
midst of an unresponsive if not a hostile population, but
by working with friendly People Movements and their
resulting churches. If we wish to leave people in darkness, then we should continue the present strategy of
the Mission Station Approach.

We Must Not Forget the Intelligentsia

"We have a mission to the educated classes of the
world," some will say. "The strong racial feelings on
which People Movements depend are much less opera-
tive among the emancipated leadership of the nations
of the world. Strict endogamy is characteristic of the
more primitive sections of the human race. We refuse
to abandon the thinking leadership of the world to their
own devices. Christ must be proclaimed to them also."

This seems a telling objection. However its force is mitigated by two considerations.

Firstly, the Gospel can be proclaimed to people only if they will listen. The thinkers, the leaders and the privileged, are as a rule difficult to reach. They are self-satisfied. They do not come to Christian meetings. They do not read Christian books. They smile condescendingly on the thought that any one religion is ultimately true. They are certain of the spiritual superiority of their national system. There is no proof at all that the Mission Station Approach succeeds in getting the intelligentsia to listen. Indeed, as far as a proclamation which issues in conversion is concerned, all the evidence is that it does not achieve it. That is to say, that the rejection of our proposal and the continuation of the present strategy would in no way assure that Christ was proclaimed to the intelligentsia of the as yet un-discipled nations.

Secondly, as Professor Arnold Toynbee points out, the religions of the proletariat tend to be adopted by the dominant minorities. This occurred during the first three or four centuries of the Christian era. The only place in all India where upper caste populations are being converted is where the "Untouchables" have previously come into the Christian fold in large People Movements, and where a degree of perfecting has taken place. In these villages the religion of the proletariat *is* being adopted by a part of the leadership in a series of small caste-wise movements. It is often said that tribal conversions mean the leadership deciding and the masses following. But another facet of this fascinating subject is that if the masses accept the Christian faith, the leadership must usually follow suit. Perhaps the conversion of the intelligentsia of the non-Christian nations of the world will not be brought about by conviction on the intellectual plane, by the compelling force of systems of Christian philosophy, but rather, as the intelligentsia observe large populations of Christians at work and at worship, they will come to their own conclusion that Christ is the Saviour. The intelligentsia must be reached. Perhaps the well-shepherded People Movement Churches constitute the best way of reaching them.

The Passing of Racialism Demands People Movements

The support of People Movements has suffered because of an aristocratic view of the races of mankind, in which some were held to be superior and some inferior. The opinion was common in India that one Brahman convert was worth many Untouchables. Church growth in Africa was depreciated because it was from "primitive peoples of limited possibilities". To-day this view is no longer tenable. Certain races because of environmental factors have undoubtedly progressed farther than others. But the facts simply do not permit us to hold that these differences in present achievement reflect an inborn structural difference.

It has been well pointed out that the Christianization of the British Isles commenced when slaves from Britain were seen in the Roman market place being sold like cattle. When the peoples of northern Europe were considered barbarians, then they were discipled. Those who have the power invariably consider themselves superior by nature. But those who are barbarians, given the perfecting processes of Christianity, invariably become superior themselves. Had the Church of the early centuries not discipled the savage tribes of the northern forests, there would have been no opposition to the northward rush of Islam. Had the Church of the twelfth century been alive to the tremendous importance of discipling the Mongol barbarians, much of Asia would not have been lost to the Muslims.

The battle to establish patterns of brotherhood between the white and coloured races of the world has been largely won in the Western churches. But some advanced younger churches still look down on the retarded peoples of their own colour, and question whether winning them for Christ is as important as winning a few individuals of the "superior" coloured peoples. "The Church will prosper more by winning even a few Watutsi than by winning whole villages of their serfs the Bahutu," said an African minister to me in Urundi. Examples of the same sort of thing could be given from India.

As the democratic and scientific view of the races of mankind widens its sway all such racial thinking will be superseded. Once it is, it will be seen that the barbarians, the slaves, the untouchables, the primitives, of to-day can provide the leaders of to-morrow. The case for concentrating resources behind People Movements will be enormously strengthened. It will be seen that the discipling of whole social units is the best way of building a powerful ongoing churches. I was recently in Ogbomasha in Nigeria and saw seven churches, each on an average costing $10,000 and seating four hundred people. The money had come entirely from the membership, and the services were led entirely by Africans. The parents of these Christians were animists fifty years ago. This is what can happen when missions turn to discipling even primitive and retarded peoples.

Results of Adopting the Dynamic Strategy

Suppose that the vast missionary enterprise, sensing the call of God in the marches toward Christ of hundreds of peoples, were to divest itself of much of the burden of its static work and turn purposefully to the service of growing churches, what results might we reasonably expect?

Evangelism would regain some of the *élan* which should characterize it. It would bring sinners to repentance and create new congregations. It would experience power beyond anything we can ask or think. It would share in the victories of the early Church. It would be at work discipling the "Nations".

Missions would plan for the education of the children of the growing churches. They would probably adopt the principle of helping only those growing churches which themselves helped to support their own schools. Such education would strive not so much to bring the latest Western techniques to the East, as to educate the children of the growing churches in ways which would further promote the discipling of the peoples and the perfecting of those already discipled. Thus missionary education will find its true sphere.

Medicine will enter on a new and more permanent field of service. Its main function will be to lift the entire level of health of an entire countryside. By the newer techniques of public health and preventive medicine, by the training of Christian medical men and women, as well as by the maintenance of hospitals at the centres of People Movements, missionary medicine will aid directly in the building up of ongoing churches. What it previously did for small static Christian communities, it will now do for growing churches of tens of thousands.

In *Christ's Way to India's Heart*, Pickett says that group conversions were found to improve social attitudes, produce a new scale of values for women, dissolve ancient enmities, and revolutionize ethical concepts. As these results occur in a People Movement church numbering scores of thousands, which is in intimate contact with non-Christian layers of society, there is bound to be permeation of enlightenment, brotherhood, justice and mercy which will extend across the land.

Then too the Christian revolution would become

more permanent. In Indo-China, a Roman Catholic Movement numbering 310,000 in 1800, endured almost a century of persecution with many missionary and native martyrdoms. It emerged in 1914 with a million members—just under 5 per cent of the population. Had Indo-China had merely a chain of mission stations with their gathered colony churches in 1800 it is doubtful whether they would have been able to survive, let alone advance as steadily.

Again the linkage with the world Church will be achieved in much larger measure. Most of the nationals who represent the younger churches at international conferences are products of the Mission Station Approach. Reinforcement of People Movements will raise up through the processes of education many more of their members who can become effective links and interpret to the West the Christward movements of the younger churches.

Strengthening Ongoing Christian Churches

Professor Kenneth Scott Latourette, the great historian of missions, in the last chapter of his book, *Missions Tomorrow*, says:

> If we have been at all accurate in analysing the conditions of the new day, it must be clear that the primary object of the missionary enterprise must be to strengthen the ongoing Christian communities in these lands of the younger Churches. This does not mean that the evangelization of the world or a ministry to the needs of the nation or of society as a whole should be neglected. It does mean that only as vigorous and growing Christian Communities exist can these goals be attained. . . . The rising spirit of nationalism will not allow to the foreigner the position he once occupied in the day of the advancing wave of Western imperialism and of the unchallengeable supremacy of the white man. Increasingly the determining ques-

tion of all mission programmes must be: 'What will most contribute to an ongoing Christian community?'

Dr. Latourette twice uses the word "ongoing". He does not seem to mean every small static congregation, which, given enough foreign aid, would doubtless go on. He unquestionably has in mind churches which are large and vital enough to grow. Thus his conclusions bear a considerable resemblance to our own. This resemblance is made more striking when we quote his further words:

> More and more we must dream in terms of winning groups, not merely individuals. . . . Experience shows that it is much better if an entire natural group—a family, a village, a caste, a tribe—can come rapidly over into the faith.

We have sharpened the definition of the ongoing church by pointing out the constitutional inability of the mission station churches to grow, and by indicating the very wide distribution of growing People Movements. But in any case it is agreed that the reinforcement of the ongoing church and the winning of groups to Christ is the high privilege of the missions of the future. Support should be concentrated behind these growing ongoing People Movement churches. This is to-day's strategy.

IX

IMPORTANT ASPECTS OF THIS DYNAMIC STRATEGY

Holding Gathered Colony Stations Lightly

To-day's strategy involves the continued holding of the Christian outposts, the mission stations. But they are to be held lightly. Since there are varieties of Mission Station Approach stations, let us look at two cases.

Here is one which was established sixty years ago. It now has a church of 500 souls, eighty-seven families, of whom twenty have been brought by the mission from other missions or other stations, and sixty-seven are made up of locally converted persons or their offspring. The station maintains a high school, a middle school, three primary schools, a group of five men evangelists and four women evangelists, and seven foreign missionaries. It has four missionary residences. It is considered one of the main stations of the mission. But it has probably not one chance in a thousand to bear and develop a living Christward movement. In an era when the sending churches are determined to transfer support to People Movements and to hold lightly the mission stations, what will happen to it?

The financial situation will be investigated. It will be found that the high school is nearly self-supporting, the middle school is three-fourths so, and the primary schools cost the mission more than the other two combined. This is because fees cannot be collected from

primary school pupils. The men's and women's evangelistic work cost the mission as heavily as do the seven
missionaries. It is found that by turning over the two
largest primary schools to the town authorities to maintain, closing the men's and women's evangelistic work,
and moving six of the missionaries to the more fruitful
field, about twenty families will have to seek other employment and may move away. The cost of the station
to the mission will have been reduced 85 per cent. The
headmaster of the high school, a finely trained national,
is put in charge of the educational work; a capable
pastor is installed in the church, three of the four bungalows are sold and fifteen acres of land are purchased on
which Christians will be encouraged to build their own
homes. The church realizes that evangelistic work will
be done by the church members as their normal volun-
tary duty. So, while the former touring work largely
ceases, the witness in and near the town itself largely
continues. Most of the families released from mission
service find other local employment. Only a few move
away. A static non-growing outpost has been con-
solidated and held lightly. Without appreciable loss,
85 per cent of the resources have been freed for the
support of growing churches.

However, here is a mission station fifty years old
where the main work has been and is evangelistic. There
are two missionary residences, in which live a man and
his wife, and a single lady. There is a team of seven men
evangelists and five women. Year after year they preach
to the people of the town and surrounding villages.
Converts are rare. Whenever someone is converted he
has to leave town for fear of riots and reprisals. The
married lady conducts a small dispensary both in town
and when she is on tour, and has a staff of two medical
assistants. The church consists almost entirely of the
employees of the mission and their dependants. On

Sundays a congregation of forty-five meets in a little chapel on one of the mission compounds. What does "holding mission stations lightly" mean for this kind of a station?

In such cases the missionaries and their budgets and the national workers and their budgets should all be placed behind growing Christward movements. There is no need, when people are crying out to become Christians, to spend at least $6,000 a year for the next fifty years ($300,000) trying to batter down a granite wall. That $300,000, together with consecrated life which cannot be estimated in money, will develop some Christian movement among a large section of a people. It will father scores and maybe hundreds of congregations, each one growing and expanding.

It will be seen that where a gathered colony has become a real church by turning over going concerns to nationals, giving into their hands the buildings and equipment, giving them the good will which has existed toward the missions, the mission stations are really taking a forward step. The outposts which have appeared and which have been *foreign* mission stations now become the outposts of a *national* church. Nationals who have been assistants now become directors of the enterprise. The gains through unity with the people served will be very considerable and the enterprise may well operate better than it did before.

Gathered Colony Churches and People Movements

The many Mission Station Approach churches form a significant outreach of the Christian faith into non-Christian cultures. What is to be the relationship of these churches to the ongoing People Movements which will grow more and more numerous as the years go by? Will these gathered churches be able to take part in the People Movements?

We must not under-estimate the difficulties faced by the Mission Station Approach churches which attempt to start or spread some People Movement. Yet neither must they be over-estimated. Immersed as the gathered churches are in a congeries of people, it will always be possible for them to start a People Movement or, more frequently, assist one already under way. But in addition to an earnest desire to win others for Christ there are four steps which the gathered churches must take before they can assist such growth.

Firstly, gathered churches will have to accept group ingathering as a desirable form of church growth and to learn its pattern.

Secondly, they will have to concentrate their attention on some one people which they deem most winable.

Thirdly, they must renounce a common prejudice, namely, that: "We Christians have been emancipated from tribe and caste. We are above people-consciousness. Anybody joining us will naturally renounce allegiance to his former people. He will marry into *our* community. He will have fellowship with *us*. He will remember that we are now his people." On the contrary, the normal clannishness of the new group being discipled must be cheerfully accepted and, indeed, encouraged.

Fourthly and most necessary, *enough individuals and groups of that most winable people must be converted in a short enough time and a small enough area* so that each Christian comes into the church with some of his kindred. The first three steps are of importance chiefly because they enable the fourth to be more readily taken. But whether the first three are taken or not, as soon as the fourth step occurs a People Movement church will be born.

Then, too, we note that the Mission Station Approach churches have a surplus of educated technicians. The People Movements are usually deficient in such. Why

K

cannot the abundance of the one supply the want of the other?

When the gathered churches send their own sons and daughters as missionaries to serve under the direction of the independent People Movement churches, Western missions would do well to give grants to them to encourage such sharing. Again the People Movement churches can send some of their youth to the training schools of the Mission Station Approach. Give and take between the static and growing churches will bind them together in a common enterprise and help unify the emerging national churches.

However, unification might not prove a blessing. In areas where strong gathered colony churches and weak People Movements together become a unified church, there, because of the superior educational advantages of those reared in the gathered colony churches, the leadership is likely to be composed of nationals dyed in the individualistic philosophy of the Mission Station Approach. It is easy for them to despise the People Movements, see all their problems and failures, and look on them as an unfortunate bequest of the outgoing missionaries! Unless such leadership gets the People Movement point of view rapidly, unification and devolution will prove a curse to the People Movements, and the unified church will lose its only possibilities of growth.

The Place of Union Enterprises in Disciplining Peoples

What we propose is co-operation in discipling peoples. It is necessary to distinguish between this and the type of co-operation which is now so popular among the mission boards. At the present time the missionary enterprise is enthusiastically promoting "larger co-operative ventures". As long as the underlying assumptions of the Mission Station Approach are not questioned, this appears to be very desirable. For example, there is no need for every mission to have a theological seminary. That should be a union affair. There are many similar tasks which are best done in co-operation. But our argument is that co-operation among static mission stations is a way of doing better a job that does not need to be done. We would apply the same tests to the "larger co-operative ventures" that we do to the mission stations. If they can be shown to buttress growing People Movement churches, then they have great value for missions. If they simply further serve the richly served gathered colony churches, then *every contribution to their support is being spent at the place of least return.*

. For example, let us imagine a union theological college. It admits only graduates and is one of the show places of missions. But, because the richly served Mission Station Approach churches have more college graduates we find that of the 89 students in this seminary all but 23 come from static churches. Of the 23 who are from People Movement churches, 7 intend to get into the service of large influential educated gathered colony churches. We could conclude, from a picture of that sort, that the theological college, though a union enterprise, will play no important part in discipling the peoples of that great land. Or let us imagine a mission medical college, in which out of 104 students 73 come from tribal movements to Christianity and are going back to these movements with a sense of divine call to help their own people. We could conclude that the college was playing a reasonably valuable part in today's strategy.

There are a few People Movement churches which have achieved such a size and rate of growth that their fathering mission can no longer cope with the opportunity for expansion. A second mission has been called in to help the growing churches. Both co-operate in assisting the one People Movement to develop. Such union enterprises are found in several lands and are urgently needed in many more.

For example, in Nigeria there is a small People Movement of great promise. About 2,000 out of a tribe of 30,000 have become Christian in a fashion which augurs well for rapid growth in the future. Were five families and five single ladies to be sent to that field at once there is reason to believe that the 30,000 persons would become Christian within the next fifteen years. But the mission concerned has sent only one family and insists that it can send no more.

If a one-family approach is continued, the majority of the tribe will be lost to Christianity. If the fathering mission cannot supply more than one family, its clear duty is to spend time and money in searching for other missions to help reap this harvest.

What is urgently needed in each land where there are many opportunities for People Movements is to appoint some person whose sole duty would be the constant study of the needs of the movements and the resources of the missions. He would find frequent opportunity to aid in the creation of union enterprises for the discipling of peoples. Without such appointment there is no one to steer suitable missions to appropriate openings or to challenge missions facing some huge opportunity to multiply their own resources or to call in aid.

Untapped Reservoirs

Even if the entire missionary enterprise were to become immediately convinced of the desirability of this strategy—a consummation devoutly to be desired, but hardly to be expected—it would take time for the shifts of emphases to be carried out. Moves of this kind should be preceded by careful research and consultation. In the meantime the mission stations should be regarded as reservoirs. This will give them a chance to adapt themselves to survival under changed conditions. In mission stations where the national staff has no other means of livelihood, and no land or houses, Christians can be helped to buy land, build houses, get employment, and make themselves a part of their town or village. Thus when the mission moves the church will remain firmly rooted in the soil. The existence of the great reservoir of mission resources will also help the mission boards and societies in meeting emergency calls. Recently Japan was considered, and may still be considered, a wonderfully open door. Had skilful research in 1946 indicated that great growth of the churches was possible in Japan, missionaries and resources from all over the world, from out of the great reservoir, could have been moved to Japan. Had the door remained open, they would have stayed there. Had the door swung shut, they could have been returned to the reservoir or moved on to the growing churches. It would thus have been possible to have moved 2,000 experienced missionaries to Japan within the one year 1948. As it was, the arrival in Japan of a few hundred of new inexperienced missionaries was all that the evangelical churches achieved.

New resources will surely be available once the laity come to feel that the churches on the mission field are really growing. The sending churches have resources which are ordinarily not touched. Christians like to give to work which is establishing Christian congregations, baptising sinners, planting the banners of the Lord in the hearts of multitudes and re-enacting the great People Movement recorded in the Book of Acts. As missions turn to the planned support of the churches which are reproductive, they will discover new sources of giving.

Nothing could be better for missions than a bold strategy of actively supporting reproductive churches. The machine of missions comes like all organizations to have a certain antagonism to change. The bureaucracies which operate the great automobile factories in America seldom adopt new and advanced designs until forced to do so by the success of some competitor. Bureaucracies are by nature conservative. Missions would function with new life if their aims were radically pruned and they rededicated themselves to the business of planting self-propagating churches.

Pauline Methods in People Movement Churches

The New Testament throws much light on the methods for developing People Movement churches. Paul's methods are in remarkable contrast with those followed for the most part by modern missions. Roland Allen has given to Christendom the classical statement in his most important book *Missionary Methods: St. Paul's or Ours?* Allen was impressed with the top-heavy procedure of modern missions, and he studied his New Testament to find out how St. Paul managed to establish such vital ongoing churches with such a simple plan of procedure. His findings may be briefly summarized as follows.

Paul on arrival converted men and women to faith in Christ. We never find him settling down to prepare the ground for future conversions. The resulting churches rapidly became self-supporting and self-governing. We never find Paul governing and serving a church by workers paid from foreign funds. In about six months he taught the converts the necessary elements of the faith, ordained a ministry and made provision for the administration of the sacraments. He then passes on and the church is left to grow by the power of the Holy Spirit. He occasionally visits it and writes to it, but in no case does he settle down and support it. He builds no buildings. He founds no schools. He does not attempt to give the elaborate teaching which is thought necessary in modern missions. Those things grow later out of the life of the church itself. Paul is content to *establish the churches and let them grow with the power which is from Christ.*

When we realize how the early Church rode the crest of a great socio-religious People Movement, we are ready to apply Allen's incisive analysis to to the People Movement churches of our time. Should not the methods which worked so well in People Movements then work well now? True, Paul had, in the Jewish backbone of each of the early churches, some very fine material. Judaism was a preparation for Christ of a kind which no other people has had. In consequence, we cannot blindly apply this summary of New Testament methods to all People Movements to-day. We cannot usually duplicate Paul's few weeks or months. These present-day movements from illiterate spirit or idol worshippers need education. The training of the pastorate is highly desirable. Adequate spiritual nurture after baptism is essential. A somewhat more lengthy residence of the missionary often seems advisable. Nevertheless, where group after group is being discipled in the New Testament fashion and the missionary must leave village congregations for months at a time, there many aspects of Paul's methods can be used with profit to-day.

We list some of the valuable Pauline emphases: the rapid achievement of self-government in even remote congregations; the confident surrender of the younger churches to the sometimes slow processes of the Holy Spirit; the permitting of discipline to arise from the conscience of the new church rather than to be imposed according to the conscience of the missionary; the willingness to let social improvement come from the church itself as a normal fruit of the Spirit. Missionaries assisting rapidly growing People Movements will have to follow some such methods. They cannot stay and mother each congregation. In leaving the congregation to work out its own salvation under the guidance of God and the leadership of its own sons, the missionary is following a successful Biblical pattern. Allen's books further develop these useful ideas, and should be required reading for all working in People Movements.

Church-Mission Relations

As the older churches reinforce the growing younger churches, problems of church-mission relationships will arise. When the mission serves a great growing People Movement church it readily and correctly comes under its control. It then becomes explicitly what it is now implicitly, the servant of the Church. Missionaries would then be seen not as parents doing things for immature children but as useful foreign servants of the self-directing and self-governing People Movement churches. Missionaries would be put under the direction of the national church to extend the Gospel. There is an intermediate stage, already in the past for some People Movements and in the future for others, where the leaders of the churches are brought into full partnership with the mission leadership on a basis of real equality. But this intermediate stage will pass. The relationship of the future is that of *missionary assistants, probably from several lands, accepted by fully independent national churches for the extension of the faith.*

Let us examine an actual case in the Gold Coast. The discipling of the tribes of the north is both possible and urgent. In the south there are four strong Protestant denominations: the Ewe Presbyterian, the Presbyterian, the Methodist and the Anglican. These are consciously independent and are inclined to think that they should start mission work in the north. They have not invited massive foreign aid nor have they sent up the scores of African missionaries which the situation demands. There is danger that the national churches, sensitive to their prerogatives, may discourage foreign initiative while making no adequate efforts themselves. There is also danger that foreign missions, burdened with many calls, may take refuge behind the convenient theory that "these powerful national churches simply must look after the further evangelization of their own land", and do nothing. Thus priceless opportunities could be permanently lost. What does missionary assistance to fully independent national churches mean in such a situation? Each group of churches and missions concerned must work out its own answer. Sometimes the church will survey the situation, sometimes the mission. Sometimes the main burden will be carried by the missions, sometimes by the churches. Sometimes the discipling of responsive tribes will be assigned to missionaries from abroad, sometimes to national missionaries. Sometimes one might hope that joint teams would prove feasible. To reach peoples in a critical state, and there are some who will be won now or never, the International Missionary Council might well call planning conferences.

But as a first step, the churches of the growing movements should make it a firm policy to call in aid on a large scale. The former concept that the church "belonged" to the mission that fathered it, and respectfully waited for that mission to initiate new departures, has served its day. The growing churches of great peoples, such as the Karens, Koreans and Bantus need to realize that the "fathering" missions have now become the "assisting" missions. Therefore the People Movement churches will not wait for their missions to act, but will themselves search, among the younger as well as the older churches, for aid to carry out the Great Commission. In case some assisting mission can no longer cope with the extension of the movement to the limits of the people, the church itself should call for aid from other missions. It should call loudly, for many of the older churches are drugged in the service of their mission stations. It should call repeatedly, for any process involving depth of change requires time—time for the old guards to die off.

A common relationship between churches and missions has been the financial one. The reinforcement of People Movement churches must not involve uncritical and unending Western support. If every new congregation must be provided with pastoral care at the expense of the older churches, then however great the funds they will be insufficient. Only systematic giving by the incoming congregations can properly sustain future growth. Indeed, only as the centrality of the church, the rights and responsibilities of each new congregation, and the possibilities inherent in each for spontaneous expansion are commonly accepted, will healthy growth become general. It must be seen that the functions of the Church can be carried on through the indwelling of the Holy Spirit in its membership. As the idea of the indigenous expansion of the churches becomes widely known and practised, these new congregations will become a source of income, rather than expenditure, to the evangelistic movement.

On the one hand, our policy should avoid such a fanatical devotion to self-support that essential teaching is refused converts unless they pay for it. On the other hand, it should avoid such short-sighted paternalism that new congregations are indefinitely served, and hence ruled, by foreign-paid pastors. Between these two extremes lies the safe path of the New Testament Church,

Concepts of Occupation Rethought

The new strategy involves rethinking concepts of occupation. The first such concept is that it is the duty of missions to occupy territories. The newer thought is that "it is peoples on the march which are assisted". Let us see what the new concept involves in the divided state of the churches. A people is a unity. It has a consciousness of being one. As peoples on the march are assisted, therefore, it will be the aim of the Christian enterprise to operate so that a given people is assisted only by missions whose sending churches have a similar polity and theological outlook. Thus the entire people will move into Christian faith as a unity.

A second concept has been that of adequacy of occupation. This is generally expressed in terms of missionaries per hundred thousand non-Christians. As we enter the new day and ask what will contribute most to an ongoing Christian community, *adequate assistance must be thought of in relation to the number of Christians*. With each passing decade it is becoming clearer that the further discipling of the peoples of the world will be carried out largely by the millions of national Christians. They will carry the banner of Christ to the pagans of Africa. They will carry it to the pagans of China and Japan. Missionary activity will consist in the assistance of the existing surges toward Christ. Occupation will be measured, not in terms of the number of missionaries per hundred thousand non-Christians, but of the number of missionary assistants per thousand Christians. Adequate assistance will mean that degree of aid from abroad which produces the maximum results in the discipling and perfecting of peoples.

What then is the right standard of assistance? The answer is not a simple one. There are different degrees required for the various stages of People Movements.

However, let us assume that the following standard of assistance had been adopted. It is partial, for several stages in People Movements are not even mentioned in it. It is highly simplified. But it will serve for illustration.

> Gathered colony churches—one missionary to each 3,000 souls.
>
> Completed People Movement churches—the same.
>
> People Movements of over 20,000 souls with unlimited opportunities for growth, a present rate of growth of 70 per cent per decade and as yet without a trained national ministry—one missionary to each 500 souls.
>
> People Movements like the above but with a trained national ministry—one missionary to each 1,000 souls.
>
> Young vigorous People Movements growing at the rate of 200 per cent a decade or more, numbering from 500 to 5,000 souls and located in the midst of a strategic people, with no higher trained national staff from among the incoming people—one to each 200 souls.

If such a standard were applied we should immediately discern where missionary forces were now being misused, either by being too many or too few in relationship to the Christian population. We should be able to start readjustments which gave to each type of church (whether gathered colony or People Movement) that degree of assistance which was likely to help it most.

The Social Effectiveness of People Movements

Concentrating resources behind People Movements will emphatically not mean that missions merely subserve selfish ecclesiastical organizations which have more regard for their own selves than for the welfare of the community. That would be tragedy indeed! But such an outcome is neither implied nor would it be possible of achievement even if it were consciously intended. There is no force for social change which could conceivably be greater than that of a great body of Christian clergy and laity, themselves redeemed in the inner man and in close contact with social advancement elsewhere, who would at the same time be thoroughly indigenous national leaders and workers. Even looked at from the point of view of the social gospel, when Christian missions transfer resources to People Movement churches, they are dropping the scythe to mount a reaper or are climbing from an ox-cart to an automobile. Great churches seek to bring about Isaiah's prophecy: "Prepare ye in the wilderness the way of the Lord; make level in the desert a highway for our God. Every valley shall be exalted, and every mountain and hill shall be made low, and the uneven shall be made level and the rough places smooth; and the glory of the Lord shall be revealed."

People Movements and Communism

To-day the threat of tyranny operating under the guise of Communism is seen on every hand. No one can minimize its seriousness. Russian tyranny is dangerous both to gathered colony and People Movement churches. Once it comes to power it subordinates the church to its own national policies.

Two lines of action are called for. Firstly, we should educate the leadership of both types of churches in the basic tenets and methods of Communism and show how these can be combated. Secondly, we should list all those responsive peoples who during the next thirty years will become either Christians or Communists. Of these peoples some will almost certainly be lost to Communism: we think of the animistic tribes in southwest China. Some can equally certainly be won for Christ: among these are those peoples in Formosa who are now turning to Christ in chains of families. These latter should be heavily assisted now. The threat of

Communism should not frighten us into timid tentative action. Rather let it spur on to bolder efforts and more effective nurture of those peoples who can now be won.

The Time Is Short

We live in a time of revolutionary movements in Asia and Africa. Changes can take place quickly which will be difficult to make when once the shape of things to come begins to harden. With the exception of the nations now helpless in the grip of the Great Tyranny, Christian movements are now free to develop. If the Eastern world continues to travel in the direction of secular governments which maintain a really impartial relationship to the various religions practised by their citizens—a modern ideal which is difficult to put into practice—the Christward marches may continue for many years. But it is dangerous to count on such continuing impartiality. The time to reinforce growing churches is now.

If the conflict with the Great Tyranny can be postponed for some years, till the Tyranny itself breaks up, then there are possibly years of peace before us during which the sending nations may be able to reinforce at their pleasure. But it would be foolish to count on a century of peace in the immediate future. The time to reinforce growing churches is *now*.

X

FINANCIAL ASPECTS

Two Missions Contrasted

In an effort to sharpen the point we are making we give an illustration. In Table I a small mission with the Mission Station Approach is contrasted with a small mission assisting a growing People Movement. This is an example of what exists all round the world, to which we are trying to draw attention. In Table II we observe what transfer of resources would mean in terms of men and money.

TABLE I

Type of Mission	No. of Christians	No. of Mission-aries	No. of Churches	Cost per Annum $	Cost per Person $	Rate of Growth %
Mission Station Approach	2,500	20	8	100,000	40	20
Growing People Movement	12,000	6	100	24,000	2	60

Certain contrasts are evident. During the decade just passed the Mission Station Approach churches experienced a 20 per cent growth in membership. This means they grew chiefly by excess of births over deaths. During the same decade the growing People Movement churches had a 60 per cent growth in membership. Since 20 per cent of this may be counted as excess of births over deaths, we find that their growth by conversions from their unconverted relatives was 40 per cent.

The churches which are growing at 40 per cent by conversions are receiving aid at the rate of $2 per annum per individual Christian; while for churches growing at zero per cent by conversions the rate is $40 per annum! This means that in the Mission Station Approach one missionary is provided for each 125 Christians; whereas in the growing People Movement one is provided for each 2,000.

What would our proposed strategy mean if applied in such a situation? The eight Mission Station Approach churches would continue to be assisted. We shall assume that the church of 2,500 has left to it, for the time being, four missionaries. The other sixteen are moved to the growing People Movement Mission which then comes to have twenty-two. We arbitrarily leave 30 per cent of the budget with the Mission Station Approach mission and move 70 per cent of the resources to the growing People Movement mission. We now get Table II, showing what the proportions will be after the transfer has been completed.

TABLE II

Type of Mission	No. of Chris- tians	No. of Mission- aries	No. of Churches	Cost per Annum $	Cost per Person $	Rate of Growth %
Mission Station Approach	2,500	4	8	30,000	12	20
Growing People Movement	12,000	22	100	94,000	8	120

We note the changed emphases. The aid to the static churches is now at the rate of $12 per person per annum, while that to the growing churches has risen to $8. This is still "unfair", yet for the time being is probably wise. We note that both types of churches now have one missionary assistant to about 600 Christians. We estimate that now the growing People Movement churches will start to grow at 120 per cent per decade, perhaps more, perhaps somewhat less. Such increase has occurred time and again where missions (mostly Roman Catholic) have tried this strategy. Thus in the course of the decade it would probably occur that Mission Station Approach churches, starting with 2,500 Christians and growing at 20 per cent, would register an increase of 500 souls, and growing People Movement churches, starting with 12,000 Christians and growing at 120 per cent, would register an increase of 14,400.

If winning men for Christ and the establishment of churches is the goal of missions, then such transfers need to be considered most seriously by leaders of Christian work. We need, of course, to beware of thinking that the growth of the church can be accomplished merely by pouring in money. The Mission Station Approach will surely have taught us that lesson.

Suppose All Boards and Churches Adopted This Strategy?

Suppose the entire Christian enterprise were to transfer men and money to People Movements as rapidly as was consistent with the welfare of both types of churches, what results could we expect during the first decade? Exact figures are obviously impossible, but we can confidently affirm that such action would usher in a new era of rapid expansion. It would add hundreds of thousands, indeed millions, of new Christians, and thousands of new churches. A multitude of new territories where there is now no church at all would be sown with Christian churches rooted in sturdy peoples.

All this would be accomplished, according to our proposal, *with no greater resources committed to the total task than are already committed. Furthermore the Mission Station Approach churches would be left more liberally assisted with missionaries and money than the Growing People Movement churches!*

L

The Investment Stake: What Will Happen to It?

A mission station costs a lot. Let us take one actual example. It is a moderate-sized station with no college or famous institution. It is a typical station with a church, boarding schools, hospital, residences for missionaries and for national helpers. These have been built at various times during the last seventy years.

TABLE III

Name of Building	Cost $	Present Sale Value $	Replacement Cost $
The church	5,000	3,000	15,000
The school	20,000	40,000	50,000
The hospital	40,000	50,000	80,000
Three residences	15,000	25,000	40,000
37 quarters	11,000	18,000	30,000
20 acres land	600	6,000	6,000
Totals	$91,600	$169,000	$221,000

The mission station represents a large investment. It cost 91,600 dollars. To replace it would cost 221,000 dollars. These figures multiplied not by hundreds but by thousands constitute the investment stake in the Mission Station Approach. It is one of hundreds of millions of dollars. It is no wonder that considerations of prudence, sound business sense, and experience, counsel caution in changing from the Mission Station Approach to the following up of People Movements. Mobility has been talked about in missionary circles for many years, but the weight of capital investments has encouraged immobility. Missions are pouring more and more capital investments into existing Mission Station Approach centres of work. It will require deep conviction, in addition to some bitter experience of the transience of the property investments in institutions divorced from great growing churches, for the existing boards and missions to embark on any new course.

Our strategy does not call for selling all mission buildings and moving the proceeds to growing movements. Many of the buildings cannot be sold. The church buildings should not be sold. They belong to the local congregations even though built with foreign money. The self-supporting and nearly self-supporting schools and hospitals too should continue to operate as Christian institutions. Mission property should not be turned over to local congregations but to trustees representing the entire area. This will tend to ensure that the property will be used for the purposes for which it was given. Some buildings may be sold and the proceeds used to build anew on the fringes of a People Movement. However, it would be unwise to count on too much of this kind of money.

The older churches need to regard their present buildings on the one hand as expendable and on the other as dedicated to the business of witnessing for Christ in the places where they have been built. "We probed for seventy years", the older churches might say, "and explored a great new territory. We built the kind of a base which could have served a mighty Christward movement. However, such an exodus did not occur here. It did arise 250 miles away. We refuse to be tied down by this base to a scheme which is non-productive as regards the discipling of peoples. We shall turn this plant over to national Christian leadership under the Church. Our buildings have not been wasted. Many of them are over fifty years old. They have rendered their service—*a wonderful service*. But we shall not let them sway our thinking in the vital matters ahead of us."

The Investment Value of Missions

An investment is money expended in such a way that it creates more money. Let us look at the investment value of each type of mission.

The gathered colony approach is expensive, not merely in its original form, but in every successive expansion. To those nurtured in the Mission Station Approach, the spread of Christianity means more and more gathered colony churches with their long periods of education and service paid for by the older churches. Each new mission station means evangelism, medicine and education whose cost falls on the mission. The part which the new congregation bears remains very small, for it takes perhaps fifty years for the colony to be transformed, at mission expense, into a church which with difficulty supports one full-time pastor! Thus the investment value of the Mission Station Approach is low. It does not and cannot succeed in planting churches which in relationship to the fathering mission will, in the forseeable future, begin to approximate to even equality of effort.

People Movements, on the other hand, from the beginning both support their own catechists and have promise of a respectable income as the wealth of their large membership grows. Opportunities for economic development naturally vary. They are low in the People Movements from among the landless victims of the Hindu system. They are high in those in the rich expanding lands of Africa. But this is the age of the common man. Governments labour to raise the standard of living of their poor. As this rises, the income of the churches will rise. One has only to see the financial condition of the churches of West Africa, the Lushai Hills, Sumatra and the Philippines to see that, for People Movements, missions are not committed to unending outlay but are in the nature of a priming of the pump. They create numerous self-supporting and self-propagating churches. The investment value of People Movement missions is high. They succeed in planting churches which, in relation to the fathering missions, will, in the foreseeable future, relegate foreign aid to a minor position.

Financial considerations are important. They are solidly in favour of switching to missions with a high investment value.

XI

RESEARCH IN GROWTH

If we are to advance in the business of our Master, in carrying out the Great Commission, and planting self-propagating churches, we must define our objectives, and measure our achievements. There is now sufficient missionary experience to make that possible. Standards of achievement can be drawn up so that the sending churches may judge of the success of their ventures. Yet all this will require carefully directed investigation. We need to know a great deal more than we do.

Unexplored Areas of Knowledge

Where is real People Movement growth taking place? There is at present no division of churches into People Movement and gathered colony categories. Annual returns are not made that way. Furthermore, all the missionary returns of a given country or mission are likely to be lumped together. This covers up growing church figures in a welter of information about non-growing churches. For example, we read that the Roman Catholic population of China doubled between 1914 and 1939. This means an increase of about 35 per cent a decade. For hundreds of congregations to achieve an average growth of 35 per cent over two and a half decades, there must have been some growing at much more than 35 per cent. This probably occurred in People Movements, though, snowed under in general figures, it is impossible to ascertain. In how many places throughout the world are there People Movements growing at 50 per cent per decade or more? No one knows. Here is a tremendously important and totally unexplored field.

Can growth be forecast? Is it possible to study a church, its ministry, its unsaved relatives, its degree of church attendance, its enthusiasm for the Lord, its integration with its surroundings, the number of bridges to other peoples which it possesses, and then to forecast the amount of growth which will likely take place in the coming decade? It should be possible. It would be worth millions to the missionary enterprise.

What is the normal degree of increase of a live movement? What degree indicates healthy life? What degree indicates dangerously low vitality, malnutrition or exhaustion in the face of opposition? Christian missions do not have sufficient facts on which to base standards of normal expectation. We estimated in Chapter VIII that 50 per cent per decade was a good norm for growth. But this was an estimate. The missionary enterprise needs knowledge.

How can the fire of faith be carried from the "Jews" to the "Greeks" to-day, from a people being discipled to other as yet untouched peoples? How can these offshoots be tended so that they will achieve maximum growth? We shall be answered with many surmises, guesses and theories. But the Christian enterprise must not proceed on surmises and guesses. It must know.

What are the causes of arrest in People Movements? Why has this one stopped after reaching the thousand mark, and that one after reaching the ten thousand mark? Is it better to let a movement grow as furiously as it will and then proceed with perfecting? Or is it better to allow only moderate growth and perfect as one goes along?

How highly trained should be the ministry for illiter-

ate first generation churches? What has been the nature
of the few People Movements among the intelligentsia?
What concentration of missionaries provides maximum
growth? Can nationals, who have grown up in the
gathered colony approach, become effective leaders of
People Movements? What educational emphases enable the educated youth of People Movement churches
to keep close contact with their unconverted relatives?
What kinds of worship lead illiterates to share our
Lord's passion for the redemption of their peoples?

Here are vast areas of knowledge almost uncharted.
Of real knowledge there is a pitifully small amount.

Controlled Experiments

In the search for knowledge our minds turn to con-
trolled experiments. At present these are not being carried on. Each leader presses forward with the best that
he can do for his membership. He may use some new
technique but, since there is no setting up of the experiment, no definition of objectives, no control group and
no accurate account of results, at the end of the day the
missionary enterprise does not know much more about
discipling than it did before.

For example, does the discipling of peoples proceed
better if the first task after baptism is to make 20 per
cent of the adult population able to read their Bibles
and use their hymn-books? Or is it preferable to use an
equal amount of men and money in trying to give the
entire illiterate church deep personal knowledge of and
dedication to the Saviour? For such a study two groups
of new churches would be chosen in which all other
significant factors were about the same. In both groups
ordinary pastoral care would be given. In one group
ten thousand dollars would be spent to lift literacy
within a two-year period to the place where 20 per cent
of the new Christians could read. In the other group

ten thousand dollars would be spent in greatly increased visitation, pastoral care, instruction, worship, conference, revival meeting and the like. Measurements would be taken before and after the two years to record the effectiveness of each technique in producing genuine Christian life and sincere enthusiasm for the spread of the Good News throughout their own people. With a budget of over a hundred million dollars a year going into Christian missions, would it not be worth while knowing—not guessing—which of the two procedures gives better results?

There are many other situations where techniques now being used (without perhaps being called techniques) could be tested while being used. This could be done with little further cost once the concept of research in growth seized the minds of the leaders of missions. It would give us enormously valuable information.

Institution of Research Necessary

Research on all kinds of People Movements should immediately begin. It will take money but its cost is a legitimate charge on church and mission budgets. Any big business considers money spent on research well spent. The proposals of this book are so new that there will be much opposition to them. One way of meeting them is to secure the facts through careful studies. The leaders of the world mission of the Church can be convinced by facts. Hence what is called for is an extended series of factual studies of the effectiveness of missions, the growth of the churches, and the ways in which peoples have become Christian. Both missions and churches can institute such studies. Church magazines can focus attention on such research. Individual missionaries and ministers in the younger churches can carry it on. Once the point of view is established, the facts of any particular enterprise can be obtained which will enable it to be evaluated in terms of growth.

Training Specialists in Growth

Once it is granted that backing Christward movements of peoples is from now on the major function of foreign missions, specialists in growth will be trained and used as a regular part of the staff of Christian missions. We shall then look back with amazement on the groping hesitant decades of the past. Then we shall have members of many missionary staffs who have devoted adequate study to how peoples are discipled. These men will sail on voyages of fateful exploration and discovery. They will be equipped with knowledge of scores of People Movements—will know how these arose, how they were nourished by the mission-mother, how they were weaned and their ailments treated. They will know many other things which are needful for the best use of the great treasure of Christendom which is the missionary passion of the churches. These explorers will discover a new world.

XII

MARCHING WITH GOD TO THE HEART
OF THE NATIONS

A missionary recounting the initial stages of a great People Movement affirmed: "There was a tremendous sense of the Power of God through it all. We saw more miracles among the new Christians than are recorded in the Acts of the Apostles. Those were great days."

In this new era we need great days. For it is an era of great confusion. Men have lost a sense of direction and purpose. The revolutions in the lands of the younger churches bewilder Christian leaders. The terrific threat of tyranny lies like an ominous thunder-cloud across the fair landscape. Nevertheless, even in this day the Christian churches can win their most notable victories. Out of imminent disaster and widespread confusion they can contribute the only enduring bases of national well-being: great numbers of living churches which fear and love and worship the true and ever-living God. As men are everywhere vainly seeking permanence and security in transient relationships, the Christian enterprise can go quietly onward discipling the peoples and saying to myriads of new congregations what was said of old: "Thus saith the Lord God of Hosts, if ye diligently hearken unto me, this city shall remain for ever."

The dream which has created this book is a dream of the time when He shall have dominion from sea to sea and from the river to the ends of the earth, when there

shall be abundance of peace and the righteous shall
flourish, and He shall redeem the poor and needy, and
all nations shall serve Him. The faith which has penned
these pages is a faith that He who commanded His followers to disciple the nations is in these days sounding
no retreat. He is pointing with pierced hand out-
stretched to a multitude of peoples.

It remains true to-day that the God of Abraham, the
God of Isaac and the God of Jacob sees the afflictions
of His peoples which are in Egypt. He hears their cry
by reason of their taskmasters. He knows their sorrows.
And He has come to deliver them out of the hands of
the Egyptians and to bring them into a good land and
large, flowing with milk and honey. He spoke *then* to
"all the congregation" of His people. "Every family"
from "every tribe" was to seek its own protection under
the blood of the lamb; and then to wait, staff in hand,
loins girded and feet shod, for the united move out of
bondage. As God brought out an entire people then, so
He wills to bring out entire peoples *now*—out of their
darkness into His wonderful light, out of the worship
of ideas and gods of their own manufacture, into che
worship of the God of righteousness and love.

Throughout this book we have urged human considerations for the transfer of support to People Movements. But there is a divine consideration: the peoples
who can to-day be discipled consist of millions of individuals whose salvation *God wills*. That is the reason
they can be discipled. They can be brought into eternal
life in the next decade if they are invited in with their
communities. We can properly sense the call of God in
the multiplicity of People Movements which exist to-
day. *These are they concerning whom our Lord says*: "*Say ye
not, there are yet four months and then cometh harvest? Behold,
I say unto you, Lift up your eyes and look on the fields; for they
are white already unto harvest.*"

God is calling to us to use what we have. As He said to Moses so to us He says: "What is that in thy hand? Use it. I will bless it to the bringing out of the people." We are accustomed to calls to new and difficult tasks for which great new resources are required. But this call to mass resources behind growing churches is one to be answered with what we have already in our hands.

As the mission station churches already established begin to share in the victories of the Cross in People Movements to Christ, they will experience a revival of their own faith. These educated churches will probably be the first exterior Christian churches to be visited by the members of the less educated People Movement churches. The mission station churches will probably exercise a broadening and steadying influence on them. These sturdy orthodox outposts of Christendom will rally the People Movement churches in many a time of hesitation and divided counsel. The mission station churches have been no mistake. God has planted them. They will play a vital part in the establishment of a Christian civilization transcending the limitations of race and clan. They will mightily assist in ushering in an era of universal brotherhood. Perhaps as the People Movements give them a growth that they alone cannot achieve, they will give the People Movements a wider Christian outlook. We believe that both types of churches in the victorious days that lie ahead will grow together into one living universal Church.

George Fox, at the beginning of that great People Movement which soon brought one in a hundred of the population of England into the Society of Friends, had a vision in which he saw "an innumerable company, as many as motes in the sun, which shall come to the One Shepherd and the One Fold".

It is given to all of us to see that same vision. Not in

England only, or in Africa only, but in almost every country of the world, an innumerable company, shall come to the One Shepherd and to the one sheep fold.

The Great Century of Christian Missions may well be followed by a Greater Century of the Christian Churches. As the churches of Christ all round the globe, the older churches and the younger churches banded together, recognize the primacy of discipling those peoples who have been called of God, and as these churches resolutely refuse to be turned aside from this harvesting of the ripened grain, there may well result a century of expansion such as has not yet been seen. From a human point of view we advocate a winning strategy of missions. But from God's point of view we are invited to march with Him down an ever-widening avenue to the hearts of the nations.